not just ned

a true history of the Irish in Australia

First published 2011 by National Museum of Australia Press

PO Box 1901 Canberra ACT 2601 Australia
Telephone +61 2 6208 5000 Facsimile +61 2 6208 5148
nma.gov.au

National Library of Australia Cataloguing-in-Publication entry
Author: Reid, Richard
Not just Ned: a true history of the Irish in Australia/Richard Reid.
1st ed.
ISBN: 9781876944827 (pbk.)
Subjects: Irish – Australia – History.
Irish – Australia.
Australia – Emigration and immigration – History.
Ireland – Emigration and immigration – History.
305.89162094

Publications manager: Julie Ogden
Editors: Thérèse Weber and Robert Nichols
Designer: Po Sung
Copyright: Denis French

Printer: Blue Star Group (Victoria) Pty Limited

Paper: Sovereign Hi-Bulk Art Board 400 gsm supplied by KW Doggett
is ISO 14001 EMS accredited and manufactured using pulp sourced
from responsibly managed forests. Sovereign Silk A2 170 gsm supplied
by KW Doggett is FSC certified, ISO 14001 EMS accredited and
manufactured with elemental chlorine free pulp.

Typeset in Mrs Eaves, Perpetua and Candara

Object photography: Don Brice, Dean Golja, Judy de Man, Murray
McKean, Peter Melville, Bryan Rutledge, National Museum of Australia
photographers Jason McCarthy and George Serras, and lending
institution photographers

Not Just Ned: A True History of the Irish in Australia, an exhibition at the
National Museum of Australia, 17 March – 31 July
Senior curator: Richard Reid
Curators: Cinnamon Van Reyk, Rebecca Nason and Karolina Kilian

Cover: Monstrance made from jewellery donated by Brisbane Catholics
for the Cathedral of the Holy Name 1928 (detail)
St Stephen's Cathedral, Brisbane
object photograph by Peter Melville

Previous page: *Emigrants Arriving, Sydney Harbour, N.S.W.* 1853
by Oswald Brierly
National Library of Australia

contents

Ambassador's message

Fáiltím go fonnmhar roimh an taispeántas seo ar na Gaeil san Astráil. I very much welcome this exhibition on the Irish in Australia by the National Museum. It is a tangible and fascinating acknowledgement and tribute to what has been a distinctive and defining contribution by the Irish to the building of the Australian nation. Nowhere in the Irish diaspora have our people so influenced the personality of a nation than here in Australia.

I remember from my first arrival in Australia seeing so many familiar Irish faces looking back at me from the crowd, reflecting the enormous contribution we have made to the gene pool. The Irish came in huge numbers, constituting about 30 per cent of the settlement during the formative first 150 years. They came as convicts – including the captive patriots of several Irish rebellions and of agrarian dissent – free settlers and refugees from famine and oppression. They were determined to make their way in this lucky land of opportunity and escape from marginalisation in their homeland. Not always welcomed by an establishment harbouring old country prejudices, the greater number came in at the lower rungs of society and, to their great credit, went on to triumph and advance over the years. Retaining a residual unease with the Empire and connections with Britain, they grew in confidence and comfort in their adopted land, in tandem with the growth of Australian nationalism and a distinctive Australian identity.

In Australian history the Irish were very much to the fore in opposing injustice and championing freedom and the rights of man. This manifested itself at times in violent opposition. The homesick convict rebellion at Castle Hill in New South Wales in 1804 was essentially the final battle of the great Irish rebellion of 1798. An equally violent but more substantive event, with enduring consequential reforms, was the rebellion at the Eureka stockade, which involved many nationalities but was Irish-led and comprised largely Irish diggers. In subsequent years, the Irish demand for fair play under the Southern Cross would be advanced through the trade union movement and the Labor Party, both of which were strongly influenced by Irish Australia.

As one of the Irish who stayed at home to push the boats out to Australia, Britain, the United States, Canada, Argentina and the other diaspora counties that are today home to more than 70 million people of Irish descent, I value highly and acknowledge with pride the continuing links between Ireland and the global Irish family. Over two centuries, the cause of Ireland has had its faithful supporters here in Australia. The major events in the Irish struggle for freedom have had their parallels here. The 1798 rebels; the Young Ireland intellectuals William Smith O'Brien, John Mitchel and Thomas Francis Meagher; and the Fenians who arrived aboard the *Hougoumont* were all transported to Australia and went on to form part of the Australian and the Irish stories. The escapes of Young Irelander John Mitchel, and later of John Boyle O'Reilly and of the military Fenians on the *Catalpa*, were sweet victories that served to sustain the Irish spirit at

7

home in years of near despair and helped inspire new generations in the renewed struggle for Irish freedom. The Irish cultural and republican revival of the early 20th century had its strong adherents here, where men like Archbishop Mannix were real players in the Irish struggle. Irish-Australian engagement with the Irish national question continues to the present day, with Australia and Irish-Australians having played a key role in the search for peace and reconciliation in modern Ireland.

Today ties of kinship and other links between Ireland and Australia remain vibrant. More than 20,000 Irish backpackers are in Australia at any one time. Even in the days of prosperity in Ireland, the Australian lifestyle, climate and culture continued to tempt Irish immigrants. A vibrant two-way tourism and a strong and growing economic relationship further strengthen the ties of kinship between Ireland and Australia.

This exhibition will help rekindle, or reinforce, the sense of Irish heritage in Australians of Irish background. It will later travel to Ireland, where we take great pride in, and inspiration from, the successful contribution our people have made in their adopted lands, not least in Australia, that most Irish of countries.

Máirtín Ó Fainín
Ambassador of Ireland

(following page) **'Digging and bagging potatoes', the Warrnambool potato harvest** 1881
State Library of Victoria

Director's message

Many of Australia's greatest stories are Irish stories. The long foundation saga of the transportation of convicts, the Eureka rebellion, the nation-galvanising fate of Robert O'Hara Burke and his companions, the nation-dividing debate over conscription in 1916, the anti-authoritarian strain of the Kelly gang and the civic idealism of Redmond Barry are just a few of the many threads that are a part of our national fabric.

The history of the Irish in Australia is the type of history the National Museum of Australia is ideally placed to tell. One of the Museum's important roles is to bring the past to life and connect it with the present. And true to this idea, this exhibition doesn't leave the great story loosely dangling in centuries gone, but brings it right up to today.

To develop an exhibition of this magnitude we have used our network of national and international museum partners to secure the loan of many significant objects and the Museum is grateful to them all. I would like to thank all of the individuals, associations, museums, libraries and archives who have generously lent prized collection items for this exhibition.

I would also like to acknowledge the enthusiastic support we have had from the Ambassador of Ireland, His Excellency Máirtín Ó Fainín, and his staff at the Embassy of Ireland, and the Australian Irish community far and wide.

This publication goes a long way towards fulfilling a need in the community. It recounts the areas of national life in which Irish Australians have been significant and links these areas of activity to people and objects. It also provides a lasting record of an important exhibition that throws light on this essential dimension of our nationhood.

Andrew Sayers
Director, National Museum of Australia

Sister of Charity, Sister Maurus Tierney, serving food to unemployed men near St Vincent's Convent, Potts Point about 1940
Congregational Archives of the Sisters of Charity of Australia

(following page) **Mary's Mount (Loreto College) orchestra, with three girls in the second row holding Irish harps** 1903
Loreto Province Archives, Ballarat, Victoria

Orchestra M...

ij's N^{t.} 1903.

The Irish in Australia: exhibition overview

About the Irish in Australia there are always opinions, some favourable, some not. Poet and storyteller Henry Lawson said that, when in trouble, he always had two friends, and one of them was an Irishman. Visiting Adelaide in the 1870s, Richard Twopenny found to his dismay that four out of five servants were Irish – 'liars and dirty'. Once accused of being opposed to Irish immigration in the 1840s, leading New South Wales politician William Charles Wentworth retorted that this was a lie: 'some of the best blood in my veins is Irish'. A couple of decades later the so-called 'Father of Federation', Henry Parkes, argued that 'Irish Roman Catholics' were not the 'best people' for the developing colony of New South Wales, and that the numbers arriving at colonial expense should be restricted. Much later, in the 1960s, Donald Horne wrote of his Muswellbrook childhood as one in which local Catholics, the great majority of whom would have been of Irish descent, were perhaps 'not quite human'. So where do the Irish fit into the Australian story?

Irish-born immigrants and their descendants have been a feature of the Australian population since the arrival of the First Fleet in New South Wales in 1788. Their influence upon, and contribution to, Australia's ever-changing and evolving cultural, economic, political and social life was of central significance. This stems from the fact that the Irish and their descendants formed a large segment (somewhere between 20 and 30 per cent) of the population up until 1914, and some suggest well beyond that. Before the large-scale continental European and English immigration of the post-1945 decades, Australia has been described as a 'fairly faithful mirror of the early nineteenth century United Kingdom' of Great Britain and Ireland, where the Irish formed a third of the population. Australia remains the most Irish country in the world outside Ireland.

What was the impact of this large Irish presence? Some Irish and Irish-Australian commentators, stung perhaps by the Establishment's relative indifference to and resentment of the Irish, especially the Irish Catholics, tended to stress the Irish contribution to society in a sometimes exaggerated manner. The title of PS Cleary's book, *Australia's Debt to Irish Nation Builders,* published in 1933, says it all. John Francis Hogan also emphasised 'Irish achievements in the land I love so well' in his much earlier work, *The Irish in Australia*, written in Melbourne in the 1880s. Hogan was a true Irish colonial: born in Ireland in 1854, he arrived in the booming 'gold' colony with his parents as a two year old.

Looking towards the bicentenary of European settlement in 1988, Patrick O'Farrell produced his own view of the role of the Irish in Australia. Rejecting the celebratory approach he discerned in Hogan's and Cleary's books, O'Farrell produced the much more sweeping claim that it had been the Irish Catholics, by opposing the dominant Protestant English and Scottish colonial ethos, who were the galvanising force behind the development of a new Australian identity and society. In particular, he had in mind the determination of Irish Catholics to have their world view incorporated into whatever it might mean to be 'Australian'. In a more cautious vein, Oliver MacDonagh claimed that a study of Australia without its Irish component 'might not be quite Hamlet without the Prince of Denmark. But it would certainly be a shallower and a poorer play'.

The Australian story would surely be a 'poorer play' without the echoes of transported exiles of Erin 'bound down by iron chains'; the orphan immigrant girls of the Great Famine of 1845–50; the Eureka rebellion's Peter Lalor; the Kelly gang; the potato farmers of Koroit; the tragically flawed explorer Robert O'Hara Burke; the founder of Victoria's State Library, Sir Redmond Barry; female educator Mother Mary Gonzaga Barry; Australia's first cardinal, Patrick Francis Moran; engineer Charles Yelverton O'Connor; anti-conscription leader Archbishop Daniel Mannix; the pastoral Durack family; and a host of others.

To date, the Irish-Australian story has been told by historians, novelists, poets and balladists. They have defined its outline, mapped its general landscape and identified its key players. Now, to bring the Australian Irish story to a present day audience, the National Museum of Australia has assembled an array of objects, documents, paintings, drawings, photographs, recorded voices, songs and moving images. The scope and suggestiveness of this material defy easy description. Some of the objects on display clearly support broadly accepted views on the Irish; others challenge some of the narrower definitions of who or what qualifies as 'Irish' in an Australian context. Represented here are, in O'Farrell's words, 'all sorts and conditions of men and women' from Ireland who, between 1788 and the present, travelled to the far side of the world as convicts or free government-assisted immigrants or passengers paying their own way.

The key element in the initial Irish experience of Australia was getting here. Until the end of the nineteenth century, the Irish journey to Australia was largely made under governmental supervision, either in a convict transport or in a vessel chartered by a colonial government. While there were some disastrous convict voyages, and later some equally appalling government-sponsored immigrant voyages, by and large the long sea passage was experienced under conditions markedly superior to those endured by many other emigrants during the nineteenth century. Even where modern Irish memory recalls death- and disease-ridden 'coffin ships' heading for North America during the years of the Great Famine, colonial government emigrants were, by the standards of the day, generally well fed, adequately clothed and medically cared for.

While the most significant years of Irish emigration to Australia were over by the time of the First World War, the Irish have continued to arrive here in smaller numbers up until the present day. Once in Australia they toiled to make a decent life for themselves and their descendants, and for the general society around them. They were involved in the creation of this new colonial society from the very beginning. Take, for example, their involvement in political life.

In the mid-1850s, on the goldfields of Victoria, Irish diggers, along with the English, Scottish and men of many other nationalities, insisted on their rights to full democratic participation in colonial life, rights long denied to them by the particular social, religious and economic repressiveness of British rule in Ireland. It was the Irish, with their symbolic password 'Vinegar Hill', their making of pikes and their leader Peter Lalor, who were arguably the most prominent contingent among the 150 or so diggers who bore the brunt of the police and military attack on the Eureka stockade on 3 December 1854. The Australian achievement of male suffrage during that decade admitted Irish males into full participation in colonial affairs; as a result, Irish Catholics such as Charles Gavan Duffy, John O'Shanassy and many others were able to reach high political office, something that would have been barely conceivable in the other parliaments of the British Empire at the time.

Even a cursory examination of those Irish who have clearly contributed to Australia's economic and cultural development produces a long list. Many of the thousands of Irish immigrants were highly qualified, as evidenced by their success in manufacturing, agriculture, pastoralism, the law, science, medicine, prospecting, engineering and many other walks of life. A surviving Union combine harvester, built in 1898, is a reminder that it was Irishman James Morrow who produced Australia's first viable combine harvester. The Lennon Foundry, founded by Irishman Hugh Lennon, was the largest of its kind in Victoria, and it was the mould boards from Lennon ploughs that the Kelly gang beat into Australia's most famous suits of armour. A significant number of colonial governors and senior members of the judiciary were Irish, among them Sir Richard Bourke, the Earl of Belmore, Sir John Madden and Sir Redmond Barry. The contribution of the Irish-born and their descendants to Australian culture generally – to literature, music, sport, the theatre, filmmaking and art – was considerable and continues to this day. The Irish, as one ballad has it, 'gave us our songs to sing', and the Australian folk music scene provides plenty of evidence of what that genre owes to Ireland.

Most nineteenth-century Irish immigrants, however, especially the Catholics, gained employment initially in domestic service and in the dozens of lowly labouring occupations that made up the urban and rural workforce. They came from fairly impoverished rural regions and possessed few skills beyond some basic literacy. It was their children and grandchildren who rose up through the ranks

of Australian society. Nevertheless, the Irish of all denominations spread across the continent and nowhere did they form the type of ghetto communities that were such a feature in American and British cities. Some locations, such as Koroit in Victoria, Kapunda in South Australia and Kiama in New South Wales had disproportionate numbers of Irish settlers, but virtually every community in every colony had its Irish component.

The descendants of the Catholic Irish often feel that their ancestors were victims in Australia of continuing British Protestant bigotry and discrimination. Phrases like 'No Irish need apply' or 'No Catholic need apply' spring to mind here. Informal employment practices that did exclude Irish Catholics from certain workplaces certainly existed well into the twentieth century. Yet, the full story here is still unclear. Recent research shows that at the census of 1901 Australian Catholics, the overwhelming majority of them Irish or of Irish descent, were fairly evenly spread through all occupational groups, with the exception of high finance. Oliver MacDonagh, quoting 1933 census figures, has shown that by that time Australian Catholics were proportionally spread through all income levels in Australia. If the Irish and their descendants, he argues, lagged economically behind the English and the Scottish, it was 'only by one or two steps'.

If the Catholic Irish felt themselves discriminated against, there was a segment of Australia's population that was far worse off than they were – the Indigenous people. The engagement of the Irish with Aboriginal and Torres Strait Islander peoples is a largely unwritten story. Some are inclined to see it as one where already downtrodden Irish Catholics must have enjoyed a fellow feeling with a similarly oppressed people. There is little evidence to support this, however. The frontier violence that marked European–Aboriginal relations, in all regions of initial contact since 1788, had its Irish participants. But there are individual instances of more positive encounters, such as the work of Irish-Australian anthropologist Frank Gillen in central Australia between 1875 and 1903. One journalist recently wondered why the exploits of sporting heroes and racehorses are more celebrated than that of such 'ethical and visionary white men' as Gillen. There is also the complex story of the Irish Sisters of St John of God in north-west Australia. While the sisters were implicated in the system that removed Aboriginal children from their families (the 'stolen generation'), they also believed (rightly or wrongly) in the transformative power of education. These histories are not easy, but in an age of reconciliation they must be considered within the frame of the Irish-Australian story.

While the majority of Irish immigrants, like many others, quietly worked away on the land and in towns and cities to improve their condition and that of their families, some became caught up in defining moments of the national story. As O'Farrell states, 'Where the action was in Australian history, there also were the Irish'. At times the 80 per cent or so of the Irish who were Catholic stood apart from the British-orientated majority, and opposed those who insisted that the only decent and loyal Australian was a good overseas 'Briton'. In that struggle, many commentators now see the Irish Catholics as solidly in the vanguard with those who sought a distinctively 'Australian' definition of themselves. From as early as the 1840s right through to 1921, support for the various national causes of 'old Ireland' sometimes provided such men and women with a sense of being a Catholic Australian of Irish origin — a sense that was sharpened in the late 1860s and 1870s by events that led many of their British colonial compatriots to view Irish Catholics as potentially violent, rebellious and hostile to the British Empire.

In 1868 an Irishman, described in the *Australian Dictionary of Biography* as a 'paranoic' and claiming to be a member of the 'Fenians' (a secret brotherhood dedicated to the violent overthrow of British rule in Ireland) attempted to assassinate Australia's first British royal visitor, Prince Alfred, the Duke of Edinburgh. Adding insult to injury, in 1876 the American Fenians organised Australia's first and last transoceanic prison break by snatching six Irish Fenian rebels from Fremantle Prison and sailing them to freedom in the United States on the American whaler *Catalpa*. And in the late 1870s, the outlaws of the Kelly gang rode the ranges with their unique blend of colonial Australian and poetic Irish sense of grievance. (One contemporary cartoon shows the infant Ned Kelly in his cot sucking on a bottle labelled 'Fenianism'.) The Kelly gang created a legend of the struggles of the 'common man' against the oppressions of a society whose laws and institutions grind him down. There were echoes here of 'old Ireland', perhaps, but it was a home-grown colonial fury sounding through the Australian bush, where small farmers and selectors faced off against haughty pastoralists and landowners backed by the police. Ironically, many of those policemen were themselves poor Irish immigrants.

With the arrival in 1884 of Irishman Patrick Francis Moran to be archbishop of Sydney, Irish Australia had a new kind of champion. Soon to be Australia's first Catholic cardinal, Moran announced that he was 'becoming today an Australian among Australians'. Moran's leadership between 1884 and 1911, while alive at times with Protestant–Catholic rancour and bitter sectarian feeling, was characterised by his insistence that Catholics take their rightful place at the centre of Australian society, a place to which their numbers entitled them. But he also urged his flock to value their Irish-Catholic inheritance. For him, 'Australianness' was not simply defined by the Protestant Reformation in Britain, 'Good Queen Bess', Admiral Horatio Nelson and the Battle of Waterloo. It could also draw on centuries of Irish history stretching back to St Patrick, the conversion of Ireland to Christianity and the cultural achievements of the land of 'saints and scholars'. On 24 May 1911, shortly before his death, Moran promoted an 'Australia Day' in Catholic schools in opposition to the celebration of Empire Day in state schools on that same date.

During Moran's years in Sydney, Ireland itself seemed to be moving, with significant political support in both the United Kingdom and countries of Irish settlement such as Australia, towards a form of self-government within the Empire known as 'Home Rule'. A growing sense among Irish Australians, and their Australian-born children, of the role that their own ancestors had played in Ireland's struggle for independence was made visible in the creation of such monuments as the large 1798 Rebellion memorial built in Waverley Cemetery, Sydney, between 1898 and 1902, and in the unveiling in Melbourne in 1891 of the statue of Daniel O'Connell, the Irish leader who had achieved Catholic emancipation (the right of Catholics to sit in the British parliament) in 1829. Conversely, for the Irish in Ireland, Australia was the grand model for Home Rule, the major colonies having gained that status within the Empire between the mid-1850s and the 1890s. Proportionally, more money was raised in Australia to support the Irish Nationalist Party than in the United States with its huge Irish immigrant population.

But Cardinal Moran, who emphasised Australia's position as part of the British Empire and the significance of that relationship, is now a forgotten figure. His mantle of leadership passed to one who did become a legend in his own long lifetime for, among other things, his support of an Irish republic – Archbishop Daniel Mannix of Melbourne. During the terrible and divisive years of the First World War and the fierce conscription debates of 1916–17, it was Mannix who defended his co-religionists against the charge that Catholic Australia was disloyal. It was Mannix who presented Catholics as remaining loyal to Australia even while

they looked with dismay and revulsion at the British handling of the aftermath of the Easter Rebellion in Ireland in 1916 and the subsequent Anglo-Irish War of 1919–21.

Those years are generally seen as a crisis point in Australian history, a time when anti-Catholicism and anti-Irishness was at its height, a time as bitter, rancorous and socially divisive as the now much better remembered anti-Vietnam war period of the 1960s and early 1970s. Interestingly, former Liberal prime minister, Malcolm Fraser, recently described wartime prime minister Billy Hughes's attributing the conscription referendum defeats to Mannix and the Irish Catholics as 'perhaps the worst act of any prime minister in Australian history'. Australian Catholic interest in Irish affairs, however, waned after Irish independence in 1921 and the civil war in 1922. The onset of the troubles in Northern Ireland in the late 1960s elicited some interest in Australia, but nothing like the uproar of the Mannix years. The issues at stake then were as much about the position of Australian Catholics in Australia as they were about Ireland. Mannix remained the key figure among Catholic Australians right down to his death in 1963, and it is worth noting that he is also remembered as a champion of other immigrant groups, such as the Italians facing internment in the Second World War.

What was of greatest significance during this time was the central role Irish-Australians played in the development of the Catholic Church in Australia. There is general agreement that up until the end of the Second World War, and well beyond, the Australian Catholic church was essentially an 'Irish' Catholic church. Irish clergy were prominent in Australian Catholic history from 1800 to the 1870s, but the key diocese of Sydney was in the hands of English Benedictine bishops. The Irish lobbied hard to have an Irishman appointed there, and they succeeded with the coming of Moran in 1884.

The following decades witnessed a growing stream of priests and nuns, the majority of them Irish, arriving to build and staff developing Catholic parishes across the continent. They were coming from an Ireland caught up, since the early 1850s, in what has been described as a 'devotional revolution' as the Irish church under Cardinal Moran's uncle, Cardinal Paul Cullen, energetically pushed through a series of ecclesiastical, educational, liturgical and clerical reforms. These same reforms worked their way through the church in Australia, producing a unified style of worship and organisation across the country that was soon simply identified as 'Irish-Catholic', although in style and appearance it owed much to European Catholic forms. Both Moran and Cullen had spent their formative years in Rome. This 'revolution' has been interpreted as an international Irish-Catholic resurgence after nearly 150 years of Gaelic Irish cultural decline, which the Catholic Church took little interest in arresting, and the gradual Anglicisation of Ireland.

Many Protestants and Empire loyalists had always looked with alarm at the growing assertiveness of Catholic Australia under men like Moran, Mannix and the other Irish-born prelates. After the attempted assassination of Prince Alfred in 1868, the Orange Order, which had come to Australia with the large number of Ulster Protestant government-assisted immigrants, grew quickly. The organisation's deep hostility to Catholicism and its admonitions to defend those bulwarks of British constitutional freedom – the King James Bible and the monarchy – appealed to many English and Scottish settlers who were alarmed by a supposedly growing Irish and Catholic threat to these institutions. While never a huge organisation, the Orange movement spread around colonial Australia, and members acted as the voice of concerned Imperial Protestantism in the face of movements like Home Rule and other perceived Catholic threats. At its most basic level, larrikin 'Orange' and

'Green' gangs brawled in Sydney's Rocks area in the 1870s. When high-profile Catholic candidates, such as Cardinal Moran, failed to gain political office, in the election for delegates to the 1898 Federal Convention, they were inclined to blame this on the Orange factor.

The Moran years, and beyond, were also marked by a great flood of building – churches, convents, schools and presbyteries – mostly achieved through the strength of financial donations from the congregations who crowded to mass Sunday after Sunday. Prominent builders were Irishmen such as Archbishop William Spence of Adelaide during the period 1915–34 and Archbishop James Duhig who ruled the Archdiocese of Brisbane between 1917 and 1965. Like nothing else, these buildings pointed to Irish-Catholic success in the colonies.

When they attended mass, parishioners heard bishops and priests, many of them with Irish accents and acknowledged leaders of the community, speak out on both religious and non-religious matters of the day. Priests were central figures in their parishes, while Irish nuns and brothers staffed and ran school systems that are still part of the fabric of Catholic Australia.

Beginning in the 1860s, the development of a separate Catholic education system, founded on the financial contributions of the faithful and the hard unpaid work of the male and female religious orders, created a distinct intellectual and emotional ambience for Australian Catholic youth. The system was developed in opposition to the colonial 'free, secular, and compulsory' state education systems introduced between the 1860s and the 1880s, and it drove a wedge between Irish-Catholic Australia and British Australia. The bishops saw the state schools as godless institutions; they wanted Catholic children to be educated in purely Catholic surroundings. There might not have been trouble over all this but for the fact that colonial and, later, state governments refused public money to Catholic schools. This meant that ordinary Catholics had to support their own schools and also help to support the public system through their taxes – a situation that produced a deep and abiding sense of grievance among 20 to 25 per cent of Australia's population.

Up until 1945 the Catholic parish, with its primary school, convent, church and presbytery, had a decidedly Irish-Catholic atmosphere and later became the hub of Australian Catholic life. Blessed with a host of distinctive characters, Catholic society found its greatest singer in 'John O'Brien' (Father Patrick Hartigan), born of Irish parents in Yass, New South Wales, in 1878. His book of verse, *Around the Boree Log*, published in 1921, celebrates the Catholic and Irish life of bush parishes, but it touched a nerve among Catholics nationwide and became a bestseller. As Australian society recovered from war, the social and political acrimony of the conscription issue and postwar divisions over Irish independence in the 1920s and 1930s, many Australian Catholics centred their non-working lives on the parish and its various social and religious institutions. The laity achieved a sense of close personal identity with the church through membership of organisations such as the Australian Holy Catholic Guild, the Hibernian-Australasian Catholic Benefit Society, the Children of Mary and other sodalities and confraternities.

The strength of this Australian Catholic lifestyle was on full view on such great occasions as Sydney's Eucharistic Congress of 1928. The event symbolised the extraordinary spiritual and institutional power and reach of a Catholic church still very much in the hands of Irish priests and prelates. Even today, it is hard to imagine Sydney streets packed with about 750,000 people waiting to see the sacred Host, at the centre of an 18,000-strong procession, carried up from Circular Quay to St Mary's Cathedral for a Congress mass. Such displays, and there were others over the years, marked the public high point of an

Irish-Catholic Australia. Leaders such as Mannix, and Moran before him, probably both alienated and angered anyone of Irish-Protestant descent in Australia with their view that to be Irish in Australia was to be Catholic, and that to be Catholic was to be Irish. Moran had done much during his rule in Sydney to convey to his flock the significance of their distinctly Irish-Catholic spiritual heritage: 'I find that the faithful entrusted to my spiritual charge have the same piety, the same love for religion, the same generosity and spirit of sacrifice which distinctly mark the old Church at home'.

When John Fitzgerald Kennedy, a Catholic and a great-grandson of Irish immigrants, was elected president of the United States in 1960, the event was hailed by the Irish in Ireland, and by the huge number of descendants of Irish-Catholic immigrants in America, as a political apotheosis. However, decades earlier the Irish in Australia had also enjoyed great political success. In 1929 Australians, by electing the Australian Labor Party to power, brought James Scullin to the office of prime minister, both of whose parents were Irish-Catholic immigrants. In the 1930s and 1940s another three prime ministers, all of whose direct antecedents were of Irish-Catholic stock, were also elected to power: Joseph Lyons (1931–39), John Curtin (1941–45) and Ben Chifley (1945–51). None of these leaders traded much upon their Irish background, although all had supported the right of Ireland to independence, preferably within the British Empire and Commonwealth. Scullin and Lyons both visited Ireland and were thanked officially by the government of the Irish Free State for their support in the struggle for independence. Curtin, as an Australian, thought the claims of his Irish ancestry bogus, but as a socialist he certainly defended Ireland's right to independence. Of the four of them, the one most caught in the trammels of Catholic Australia was Ben Chifley. In 1914 he married a Presbyterian in a Presbyterian church, thereby, under Catholic church law, excluding himself from the sacrament of communion. When he was in Canberra, however, he often attended mass at St Christopher's Cathedral and sat in a special chair at the back that became known as 'Chif's Chair'. Second-generation Irish Catholics gained positions of supreme national leadership in Australia well before it happened in the United States.

As the twentieth century wore on, old hostilities began to fade – especially after the Japanese threat to the nation during the Second World War, which helped to unite Australians across previously denominational and ethnic boundaries. Interest in such matters as Irish reunification, a cause espoused by prominent Irish leader Éamon de Valera during a nationwide tour in 1948, was negligible. Patrick O'Farrell even entitled an analytical article on this visit, 'Irish Australia at an End'. Postwar migration from Catholic countries other than Ireland began a process whereby the hold of the Irish in the Catholic Church began to erode, a process that the growth of an Australian-born priesthood had foreshadowed even before the war. Today's Irish immigrants are few in comparison to the large numbers in previous centuries and could not hope to have the same formative influence on Australian society as their predecessors. But some have made a name for themselves with significant contributions to the nation's cultural and social life. One such is Claire Dunne, who co-starred in the film made from John O'Grady's whimsical story of ethnic Australian social mores, *They're a Weird Mob*. Dunne went on to be the founder, under the Whitlam government, of the ethnic radio stations 2EA and 3EA.

Old divisions over Ireland rumbled on, however, throughout the 1950s and 1960s. In particular, Australian governments under Sir Robert Menzies were unwilling to recognise the claim of the Dublin-based government of the Republic of Ireland to jurisdiction over the whole country, including the six counties of Northern Ireland, which were still an integral part of the United Kingdom. But in 1963, when Menzies brought in a form of state aid to Catholic schools and then, two years later, appointed a full-time Australian ambassador to Ireland, he was perhaps signalling an end to those issues about Ireland and religion that for so long had divided Australians. Politics perhaps played a part, since the Catholic vote, long seen as being more likely to favour the Australian Labor Party, was now just as likely to be given to more conservative parties.

Over the past 30 years, native-born Australian engagement with Ireland has largely been with the cultural aspects of an Irish heritage. Television mini-series such as *Against the Wind*, *Brides of Christ*, *The Harp in the South* and *The Last Outlaw* brought the stories of Irish Australia to a wide popular audience. The nationwide family history movement grew strongly in the 1980s and put many in touch – some for the first time – with the reality of their ancestors' Irish background and their journey to Australia. This was made possible by the generally excellent Australian archival records. A dedicated few have even taken up Irish language classes. Following the folk music revival in both Ireland and Australia in the 1950s and 1960s, Irish traditional music of all kinds has become a significant part of the Australian folk music scene, and recent scholarly efforts have begun to unravel the connections between Irish and Australian music. From about the 1980s, being Irish became almost fashionable in Australia, and by the 1990s the international phenomenon of the 'Irish pub' took hold in Australian capital cities. The historical significance of the large Irish presence in Australia in former times, however, seems almost forgotten except by a few researchers. Only on one day of the year are the Irish clearly visible to all – St Patrick's Day.

St Patrick's Day activities in Australia have mirrored the changing nature of Irish Australia. In the early years of the penal colony of New South Wales, convict workers, hungover from the excesses of the patron saint's festival, were remarked upon by their British gaolers. During the middle years of the nineteenth century, the day was often celebrated with community dinners and lengthy speeches, and was attended by Irish and non-Irish alike. After the Fenian scare of 1868, St Patrick's Day celebrations often took the form of large picnics with music, dancing, and semi-serious sporting activities (such as the tug-of-war). In Sydney, by the 1880s, street marches were held. But by this stage the day was definitely an Irish-Catholic occasion. In the mid-1890s, Cardinal Moran, feeling that the event was too closely associated with loud, unedifying activities that tended to strengthen prejudices about Catholics, took matters into his own hands. He developed Sydney's St Patrick's Day as a 'national festival' to be celebrated by appropriate religious ceremonies in the cathedral, Catholic school athletic demonstrations at the showgrounds, a vice-regal lunch and a formal concert in the Town Hall. In the crisis years of 1916–22, St Patrick's Day parades in Melbourne under Archbishop Mannix were assertive political statements of Catholic loyalty to Australia during the war and support for the cause of Irish independence. During the 1930s in Sydney, with Irish-born archbishop Michael Kelly supervising affairs, the parades had no such Irish political content: instead, floats displaying stories of early Catholic Sydney or St Patrick himself, surrounded by round towers, harps and Celtic crosses, took centrestage. After the Second World War, however, the city's observance of St Patrick's Day amounted to little more than special religious services, an evening concert and school sports displays at the showgrounds. For as long as Mannix was alive, the Melbourne parade continued, but it ceased altogether in 1970. Could this perhaps be explained by a growing sense among a generation of postwar Catholics, as sectarian antipathies slowly evaporated, that these public displays of Irish ethnic origins carried less and less meaning for them as Australians?

The parade experienced a rebirth in Sydney in the late 1970s, and a patchy revival in Melbourne, organised by Irish ex-pats as a fun day of celebration and fancy floats with an Irish cultural emphasis. Virtually absent was any reference to previous Irish-Australian stories and that sense of Catholic self-assertiveness characteristic of earlier parades. It all seemed very much part of a new multicultural Australia, of which the modern Irish were simply one more colourful component. One Melbourne organiser unwittingly provided an epitaph for the old-style Australian St Patrick's Days: 'It is a great day for the Irish, the English, the Vietnamese, the Cambodian and everyone else who cares to come to the party'.

Nevertheless, St Patrick's Day remains *the* Irish day in Australia. The statements of today's parade organisers might show little understanding of the complexities of an Irish-Australian past stretching back to 1788, but through all the shenanigans — green beer, dyed hair and T-shirts bearing 'Kiss me I'm Irish' slogans — a question still lingers in the air: 'What has it meant to be Irish in Australia?' The objects and stories assembled here do not provide a simple answer to that question, but rather show just what a remarkable and rich story Australia has inherited from a past where the Irish were among the stars of the show.

Richard Reid, senior curator

Larry Foley, leader of the larrikin 'Green' gang in The Rocks, Sydney, and known as 'The Father of Australian Boxing'
about 1875
by Charles Henry Hunt
National Library of Australia

featured objects

The Charlotte at anchor in Botany Bay Jan 7th 20 1788

The *Charlotte* medal

Irishman John White, surgeon-general of the First Fleet, was impressed with the forger Thomas Barrett, who sailed with him in the convict transport *Charlotte*. On 5 August 1787, as the ship lay at anchor off Rio de Janeiro, Barrett was caught passing forged 'quarter dollars' to local boatmen to pay for food. White was amazed at how Barrett had managed to manufacture these coins without seemingly having had any access to fire or the other equipment necessary for coin-making. Perhaps it was this knowledge of Barrett's skill that led White to commission the convict to engrave a medal celebrating the ship's safe arrival in Botany Bay on 20 January 1788.

The *Charlotte* medal is regarded as Australia's first colonial work of art. On one side, it depicts the ship resting at anchor in Botany Bay and, on the other, precise details, in terms of latitude and longitude,

about the major places they either passed or stopped at during the eight-month voyage.

Barrett did not survive long in the colony. After little more than a month, he was hanged for stealing food, an event recorded by White in his famous *Journal of a Voyage to New South Wales* (1790): 'Barrett was launched into eternity, after having confessed to Rev. Mr Johnson, who attended him'.

The *Charlotte* at Portsmouth, May 1787 1987 (detail)
by Frank Allen
State Library of New South Wales

***Charlotte* medal** 1788
attributed to Thomas Barrett
Australian National Maritime Museum

BARRINGTON *detected picking the Pocket of* PRINCE ORLOW *in the Front Boxes at Covent Garden Theatre, of a Snuff Box set with Diamonds supposed to be worth L. 30,000.*

Published as the Act directs, Oct.r 6.th 1790. by G. Kearsley Fleet Street.

George Barrington, prince of pickpockets

George Barrington's early life in mid-eighteenth-century Ireland has been described as 'masked by romantic versions of infinite variety', including a claim to be of royal descent. Sent to a Dublin school to prepare him for university, Barrington got into a fight with another boy and stabbed him. Punished with a flogging, he bolted with a stolen watch and some money. He took up with a group of strolling players, and was taught to pick pockets by their leader, the notorious English swindler John Price.

By the mid-1770s Barrington was well on his way to becoming London's most colourful pickpocket. He lived in great style, mixing easily with gentlemen, and just as readily stealing their purses. Although he was arrested many times, he used his connections to get acquitted. One of his most famous exploits was the attempted theft of a diamond studded snuff box, allegedly worth £30,000 – a vast sum in those days – from the Russian Prince Orlow at Covent Garden. Hauled before the magistrate, Barrington pleaded his case with such a display of emotion that the prince refused to press charges.

The Irishman's luck ran out in 1790. For the theft of a gold watch he was transported to Sydney, where his 'irreproachable conduct' eventually gained him an absolute pardon. In 1796 he was even appointed chief constable at Parramatta – one wonders if he ever arrested anyone for picking a pocket.

Barrington Detected Picking the Pocket of Prince Orlow 1790
by Inigo Barlow
Rex Nan Kivell Collection, National Library of Australia

CERTIFICATE OF FREEDOM.

No. 30/446

By Order of His Excellency Lieutenant-General RALPH DARLING, Captain General and Governor in Chief of the Territory of New South Wales and its Dependencies, &c. &c. &c.

THIS IS TO CERTIFY, that *Fourteen* Years having elapsed since Sentence of Transportation for that Term was passed on *Edward Ryan* No _____, who was tried at *Tipperary Country* on the _____ of *January 1816*, and who arrived in this Colony by the Ship *Surry* _____ *Raine* Master, in the Year *1816*, the said *Edward Ryan* _____ who is described on the other Side, is restored to all the Rights of a Free Subject under such Circumstances.

GIVEN at the Colonial Secretary's Office, Sydney, this *Twentyninth* Day of *January* One thousand eight hundred and *thirty* _____

Alex. McLeay

REGISTERED IN THE OFFICE OF THE PRINCIPAL SUPERINTENDENT OF CONVICTS.

Ned Ryan's certificate of freedom

What did ex-convicts in early colonial New South Wales carry with them to prove they had served out their sentences of transportation? Edward 'Ned' Ryan, of Galong, New South Wales, always kept about him a small red wallet, which held his folded-up 'certificate of freedom'. Ryan received this vital document in 1830, the piece of paper indicating that he was now a free man and should be treated as such.

We can learn a lot about Ryan from his certificate, which also bears his signature. He was born in County Tipperary, Ireland, in 1789; he stood 'five feet six and a half inches' (1.7 metres) high; he had a ruddy complexion, hazel eyes and 'brown hair mixed with grey'.

Ryan had been part of a group of men who had torn down a dispensary in his native parish of Clonoulty, when they realised that British soldiers were to be stationed there. Transported for this crime in 1816, along with 12 others, he left behind a wife and two children. They joined him in New South Wales 32 years later, by which time he had become a wealthy man, referred to politely as Mr Edward Ryan Esq. Indeed, so extensive were his pastoral leases that he was sometimes called 'The Patriarch of the Lachlan'.

Ned Ryan's certificate of freedom and leather wallet 1830
St Clement's Retreat and Conference Centre, Galong,
New South Wales

Wathaurong weapons

It is widely acknowledged that the development of European Australia since 1788 has occurred on land taken from Aboriginal and Torres Strait Islander Australians. Irish settlers profited as much from these acts of dispossession as any other group.

The earliest major European settlement around Melbourne, or what was then the Port Phillip district, began in the mid-1830s. Prominent among some of the early settlers who came to Port Phillip from Tasmania (Van Diemen's Land) around this time were two young Irishmen, John and Robert William von Stieglitz. They took up sheep runs near Geelong and at Ballan, 80 kilometres west of Melbourne. Robert's attitude towards those who had occupied the land before the settlers set up their runs was typical of the times: 'The general rule is, if the people cultivate or grass the land they have a claim on it, but these creatures did neither'. It was the perfect settler excuse for the expropriation of land, by force if necessary.

Unsurprisingly, the von Stieglitz brothers soon came into violent conflict with the local people. Robert, in particular, tells of going out to hunt Aboriginal people who had attacked and killed settlers. When they returned to Ireland in the 1850s, the brothers took home a remarkable collection of weapons picked up after one such expedition. Among the earliest Aboriginal material collected in the Port Phillip district, these artefacts are a reminder of the reality of frontier conflict in early Victoria.

Ballan House in 1851 (detail)
by Emma von Stieglitz
State Library of Victoria

Shield made by Wathaurong people, Victoria about 1836
National Museums Northern Ireland

Pioneer chaplain

In early colonial South Australia, Irishman Charles Beaumont Howard was known as the friend of anyone in trouble or distress. Howard was South Australia's 'colonial chaplain', an Anglican clergyman who battled to establish his church in the Adelaide bush.

Sent out with Howard on the *Buffalo* in 1836 was a temporary church. However, two or three weeks of attempting to conduct services in it after he arrived at Holdfast Bay, Glenelg, quickly proved it useless. And so, in the extreme heat of late January 1837, Howard, assisted by the colonial treasurer, dragged a handcart and sail 12 kilometres through the bush to the site of the new city of Adelaide. There he erected the sail under a tree for shelter, surrounded the structure with tree branches and rushes from the coast and held Adelaide's first Anglican services.

Howard's greatest monument is Holy Trinity Church, which he opened in 1838. But in the Holy Trinity Church collection is an object that perhaps better symbolises Howard's pioneering efforts. It is a small stained-glass window, intended for the temporary church from the *Buffalo*, and decorated with the letters 'WIVR' (standing for the reigning monarch, William IV) and the date, '1836'.

Stained-glass window from temporary church 1836
Holy Trinity Church, Adelaide

Young Ireland

Regarded by the British as traitors, William Smith O'Brien and Thomas Francis Meagher were held in high esteem by their countrymen. Both were leaders of the ill-fated 1848 'Young Ireland' rebellion, which took place at the height of the Great Irish Famine of 1845–50, and both were sentenced, as convicted traitors, to be 'hanged, drawn and quartered'. In 1849 this dreadful sentence was commuted to transportation for life to Tasmania.

Three years later, Meagher escaped on a ship to the United States, where his career became the stuff of legend. In the American Civil War (1860–65), he rose to be a general in the Union army, commanding the 'Irish Brigade'. To fight for the Union, he declared, was to fight for Ireland, since Ireland could not hope to become a republic without the support of the 'liberty loving citizens of the United States'. During the war he was presented with two dress swords by Irishmen wishing to honour his 'sterling devotion to the cause of Ireland and of liberty'.

These swords recall the name given to Meagher in Irish national history – 'Meagher of the Sword'. In 1846 this rebel had asserted that armed insurrection against tyranny was justified: 'I look upon the sword as a sacred weapon … for at its blow, and in the quivering of its crimson light, a giant nation [the United States] sprang from the waters of the Atlantic'. Meagher drowned in the Missouri River in 1867 while serving as acting governor of the Territory of Montana. His body was never recovered.

O'Brien is perhaps the best remembered of the Young Ireland rebel leaders. A member of the aristocratic O'Brien family, direct descendants of Ireland's great High King Brian Boru, he initially refused to give his word not to escape in Tasmania

and was confined, first to Maria Island and later to Port Arthur. His defiant stance was driven by the belief that to remain a prisoner would keep the cause of Ireland more directly in front of world opinion. In November 1850, however, he gave his parole and four years later received a 'conditional pardon'. This allowed him to return to Europe, but not Ireland. As he was passing through Melbourne, the colony's Irish residents presented him with a magnificent gold cup produced by a local Irish goldsmith. A carved piece at the top of the cup shows a seated O'Brien receiving a laurel wreath of victory from Hibernia, the symbolic figure of Ireland.

One of the swords presented to Thomas Francis Meagher in America 1860s
Waterford Museum of Treasures

Gold cup presented to William Smith O'Brien by the Irish residents of Victoria 1854
by William Hackett
National Museum of Ireland

Hellcat of a woman

The stories that have circulated about Irishwoman Isabella Mary Kelly are amazingly lurid. As recently as the 1970s and 1980s, tabloid articles about her feature headlines such as 'Female settler was tyrant to assigned lags', 'Wild ways of grazier Bella', 'Sex-hungry tyrant lived by law of the lash' and 'Isabella Kelly – a bitter, sadistic hellcat of a woman'. The accompanying stories are little short of libellous to her memory, one even accusing her of flogging men to within an inch of their lives for refusing her favours. Most of these accounts end with Kelly receiving her just deserts by dying as an impoverished beggar living in a cellar in Sydney's dockland in the 1890s.

The truth is less spectacular. Kelly came to New South Wales in the early 1830s and acquired land in the Manning River district. She successfully managed her property herself, becoming a noted breeder of horses. Current thinking about Kelly is that she was greatly resented for the free lifestyle she led as an unmarried woman.

In 1859 Kelly was imprisoned for perjury on the false evidence of a neighbour. Although soon released and pardoned, she never recovered physically or financially. After a number of Select Committees of the New South Wales Legislative Assembly had examined her case, she was awarded the inadequate sum of £1000 compensation. She died in Sydney in 1872, not wealthy but certainly not a beggar. Kelly is now recognised in the Manning River area as a pioneer woman of great determination and ability.

Isabella Mary Kelly's branding irons about 1830s
on loan from Geoff Boyle

Isabella Mary Kelly
courtesy Maurie Garland

The Eureka stockade

The finest thing in Australian history … a strike for liberty, a struggle for principle, a stand against oppression.

Mark Twain, writer and humorist, 1895

The Eureka rebellion came after a long period of protest against the way the Victorian goldfields were being administered. Miners objected to the high cost of mining licences, brutal police 'licence hunts', the unrepresentative nature of the colonial government and general corruption. After a vicious licence hunt on 30 November 1854, tension between the miners and the authorities came to a head. As men gathered to protest, Irishman Peter Lalor, from County Laois, came forward to proclaim 'Liberty'. Next day, Lalor led about 500 miners, beneath their flag, the Southern Cross, in an oath: 'We swear by the Southern Cross to stand truly by each other, and fight to defend our rights and liberties'. Under Lalor's command, the rebellion assumed a more Irish feel. He chose the password 'Vinegar Hill', recalling the last great battle of the 1798 Rebellion in Ireland.

Just before dawn on 3 December 1854, a force of soldiers and policemen stormed a rough fort on the Ballarat goldfields known as the 'Eureka stockade'. Inside were about 150 miners, many of them Irish like their leader. In less than half an hour, the stockade fell. Twenty-seven civilians are thought to have been killed, most in the stockade itself. Lalor himself was wounded at Eureka and lost an arm. There were many reports of official brutality. Thirteen miners, six of them Irish, were later tried for high treason, but were found not guilty. No Victorian jury would convict them.

The story of the miners' battle at Eureka quickly entered Australian folklore. In 1891 the Melbourne Cyclorama Company offered the public the story in the round, in the form of a 360-degree panoramic depiction of the Eureka Stockade, at its building at Victoria Parade, Melbourne. This surviving image shows the battle at the stockade on the morning of 3 December 1854.

Peter Lalor 1856
by Ludwig Becker
National Library of Australia

(previous page and facing) **Eureka stockade** about 1891
commissioned by the Melbourne Cyclorama Company
State Library of Victoria

SPIDER DANCE.

The Spider Dance

Of all the entertainers attracted to the Australian colonies during the gold rush of the 1850s, none left behind a reputation as amazing as Irishwoman Elizabeth Rosanna Gilbert, better known as Lola Montez. In all, Montez spent just ten months in Australia – between August 1855 and May 1856, performing on the Victorian goldfields and in Sydney, Melbourne and Adelaide. The miners loved her, reputedly throwing gold nuggets onto the stage to show their appreciation. But the *Sydney Morning Herald* described her dancing as 'the most libertinish and indelicate performance that could be given on a public stage'. So what was all the fuss about?

Montez's most famous performance, and the one which pulled in the crowds, was the 'Spider Dance'. As she swayed on the stage of the Royal Victoria Theatre in Adelaide in December 1855, her act was captured on paper by artist John Michael Skipper.

It began with Montez pretending to have become entangled in a spider's web. She then discovered one spider after another, revealing her petticoats as she tried to shake them loose, all the while dancing with more abandon and passion until all the creatures had been shaken out onto the floor, where she excitedly stamped them to death. Audiences were 'held spellbound and somewhat horror struck', but when she had finished the applause was 'thunderous'.

Spider Dance 1855
by John Michael Skipper
State Library of South Australia

Copper at Kapunda

Charles Harvey Bagot came to South Australia from Ireland in 1840, aged 52. His aim was to acquire land in the colony and settle on it as a gentleman pastoralist. However, wool prices were low in the early 1840s, and Bagot must have wondered whether his emigration relatively late in life had been worth it. One day, on his property at Koonunga, 100 kilometres north-east of Adelaide, Bagot's son, Charles, picked up a piece of rock, which turned out to be copper. The ore proved to be high-grade, and the Bagot family fortune – and that of the town of Kapunda – was made.

After Bagot's retirement as manager of the Kapunda Copper Mine in the late 1850s, the Kapunda miners and other locals were determined to honour the man who had brought so much prosperity and prominence to their town. They commissioned German-born silversmith Charles Edward Firnhaber to produce a handsome cup to be presented to Bagot. Firnhaber was obliged to use a conventional imported cup for the base, but fashioned for the lid a carved model of the Kapunda mine's above-ground machinery. On 14 November 1859 hundreds crowded into the town to see the presentation. It was reported that 'the honourable gentleman was apparently so moved that his reply was scarcely audible'.

The Bagot Cup 1859
by Charles Edward Firnhaber
Kapunda Historical Society, South Australia

Tried in the desert

There was a carnival atmosphere at Royal Park, Melbourne, on 20 August 1860. A crowd, estimated at between 10 and 15 thousand, had come to watch the men of the Victorian Exploring Expedition, with their piles of equipment, wagons, camels and horses, make their departure. Their aim was to be the first European explorers to cross the Australian continent from south to north. There was much confusion as the expedition got underway: a camel bolted; a horse, frightened by the camels, threw its rider, breaking her leg; and artists and photographers jostled to record the historic scene.

One of the artists making sketches for a bigger canvas was Swiss-born Nicholas Chevalier. In his *Memorandum of the Start of the Exploring Expedition*, Chevalier places the Irish leader of the expedition, Robert O'Hara Burke, centre-stage, perched on his horse in a heroic pose at the head of the column and waving goodbye to another Irishman, Mayor Richard Eades of Melbourne.

Burke, and his eventual co-leader, Englishman William John Wills, made a very different entry into Melbourne, in their coffins, on 28 December 1861. Both had crossed the continent, but they died at Cooper's Creek in South Australia on their epic return trek. As historian Manning Clark wrote, 'The English and the Irish had been tried in the desert and found wanting'.

Memorandum of the Start of the Exploring Expedition 1860
by Nicholas Chevalier
Art Gallery of South Australia

S U T H   W A L E S

MAP
OF THE
COLONY
OF
VICTORIA

Duffy's big map

Victoria's, and perhaps even Australia's, biggest map was commissioned by an Irish rebel, a man who was eventually knighted in 1873 for his services to the Crown. Charles Gavan Duffy, a follower of the 'Young Ireland' nationalist party in the 1840s, was arrested in 1848 and tried five times, unsuccessfully, for high treason. Ireland was then in the grip of the Great Famine, and Duffy felt that one practical solution to the problems besetting the country would be to make it possible for poor tenant farmers to buy and own their own land. Nothing came of his efforts in that direction, however, and in 1855, despairing of the British parliament's ability to improve conditions in Ireland, he settled in Melbourne.

In 1856 Duffy was elected to Victoria's first Legislative Assembly. During the second half of the 1850s, the easily won alluvial gold, which had attracted thousands of immigrants, began to run out, and a major issue of the day was what to do with this restless surplus population. In Victoria, as in Ireland, Duffy supported the idea of giving access to land to those with little capital. Farming would provide a 'healthy and pleasant pursuit' for ex-diggers who might otherwise become 'discontented and dangerous to public safety'. And for his Irish countrymen, who had been driven from the land in Ireland, Duffy saw the prospect of a 'more prosperous home on the genial soil of Victoria'.

Duffy's 'Land Act' (*The Victorian Lands Act 1862*) attempted to cater for this land hunger. In his *Guide to the Land Law of Victoria*, Duffy referred to a 'large map', hanging in Melbourne's Parliament House, which showed the distribution of land ownership in Victoria. Apart from areas unsuitable for agriculture, official surveyors identified 4 million hectares where men who had been labourers in England, or tenant farmers in Scotland or Ireland,

could become owners of the soil. Intending settlers could 'select' blocks of up to 260 hectares for a small initial sum, with the rest to be paid as rent over a number of years.

The Act failed because the great pastoralists or squatters, especially in the Western Districts, were able to evade its provisions and acquire the land for even larger sheep and cattle runs. Duffy's big map, however, survives as evidence of one Irishman's dream of a new country of small farmers, far from the oppressions of the old world, enjoying personal prosperity and freedom.

Sir Charles Gavan Duffy about 1853
National Library of Australia

(previous page and facing) **Map created for the Parliament of Victoria to show land available for selection** 1862
Public Record Office Victoria

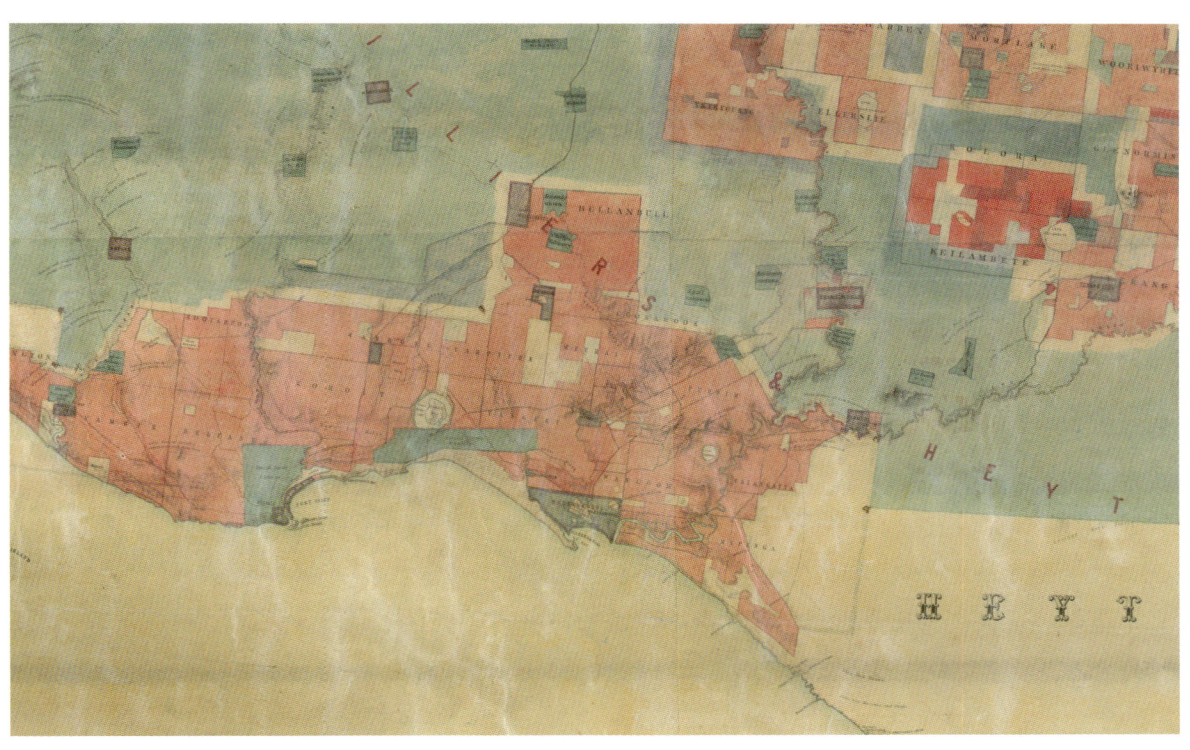

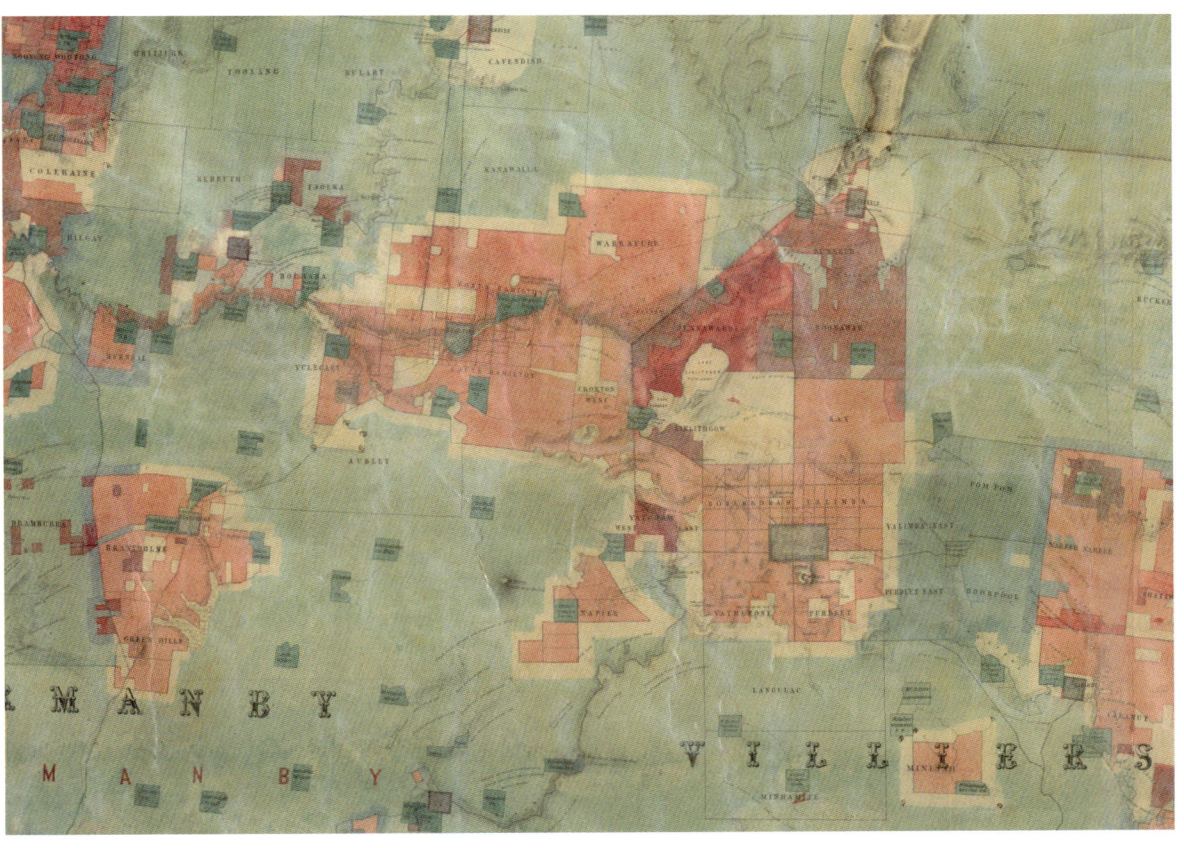

The golden probe

In Irish history Clontarf is famous as the name of High King Brian Boru's victory, on Good Friday 1014, over the armies of his Irish enemies, who were in league with Viking mercenaries. Boru, who had been trying to bring unity to various warring families and protect the country from the Viking threat, was killed in the battle. The Sydney harbourside suburb of Clontarf is undoubtedly named after the Dublin suburb that now sits on the site of the ancient battle. And it was here in Clontarf, New South Wales, on 12 March 1868, that Irishman Henry James O'Farrell tried to assassinate Sydney's first royal visitor, Prince Alfred, Duke of Edinburgh, by shooting him in the back.

O'Farrell's bullet 'entered half an inch to right of spinous process of vertebrae on a line with ninth rib, burrowing deeply into the tissues'. Whisked away to a makeshift hospital in the front drawing room of Government House, the Duke was required to remain quiet for two days. During that time a special golden probe was fashioned to enable Royal Naval surgeons to safely remove the bullet. Later, Queen Victoria showed her gratitude by presenting gold replicas of the bullet to the surgeons.

Gold probe supposedly used on the Duke of Edinburgh March 1868
Royal Prince Alfred Hospital Museum, Sydney

(left and facing) *Attempted Assassination of H.R.H. the Duke of Edinburgh at Clontarf, N.S.W.* 1868
by Samuel Calvert
National Library of Australia

The Australia House

In January 1868 the fourth Earl of Belmore, one of Ireland's leading peers of the realm, accompanied by his wife, Honoria, landed in Sydney to take up his post as the new governor of New South Wales. The couple were given a hearty welcome and quickly whisked off to Government House, where they spent the rest of the day at a formal levée, shaking hands with the colony's rich and influential citizens. Few probably paid much attention to one brief sentence in the lengthy report of the governor's arrival issued the next day: 'The four children of the Earl and Countess of Belmore were brought on shore at a subsequent hour of the day'.

For the next four years, Government House was also a family home to the four young Belmore girls: Therese, Florence, Madeleine and Mary. Lady Belmore's delicate condition, and the summer heat, led the family to a country retreat, Throsby Park in the Southern Highlands of New South Wales, and it was here that the couple's first son was stillborn. Another son, Armar, was born in Government House in May 1870. His wife's poor health, however, caused Lord Belmore to ask for an early recall to Britain, and the family left Sydney in 1872.

The people of the city thought highly enough of their governor and his wife to present the children with a doll's house on their departure. Known to the family ever after as the 'Australia House', it may have reminded them, in the cold northern winter, of the sunlight and warmth of New South Wales.

(clockwise from top) **The Earl of Belmore, the Countess of Belmore, Ladies Florence, Mary, Madeleine and Therese**
1868–70
from photograph album, 'Who and what we saw in the Antipodes'
attributed to Helen Lambert
National Gallery of Australia

(previous page and facing) **Doll's house and furniture**
about 1871
on loan from the Earl of Belmore

61

Crate full of air

In his poem 'Bogland', Seamus Heaney paints a picture of a noble but extinct creature:

> They've taken the skeleton
> Of the Great Irish Elk
> Out of the peat, set it up,
> An astounding crate full of air.

Irish settler Samuel Pratt Winter brought the enormous antlers of one of these extinct animals from Ireland back to his homestead, Murndal, in the Western District of Victoria. There they still delight and surprise visitors.

Megaloceros giganteus was the largest deer ever known; often known as the Irish elk, its range actually extended from Ireland to central Russia. The antlers would have reminded Pratt Winter of the great bogland spaces of the 'old country', where such remains were being found in the nineteenth century.

In the new world of Australia, Pratt Winter surrounded himself with visible echoes of the old world of Ireland and Europe. Well educated, this avid amateur collector was always looking for things to adorn his Australian domain. Still flourishing at Murndal is a great oak, sprung from an acorn of a tree listed in the 'Domesday Book', the famous survey of England begun by William the Conqueror in 1085. Pratt Winter also sent home to his sister, Arabella, seeds from an old cypress tree in Rome that had been planted by Michelangelo. He hoped this would allow him to establish at Murndal 'a grove in honour of a most extraordinary genius, architect, poet and sculptor'.

Antlers of extinct Irish elk
private collection

POLICE BOAT.   SHIP'S BOAT WITH THE ESCAPED FENIANS.

BARK CATALPA, C

202 TONS R

JOHN T. RICHARDSON, SHIP'S AGENT.

DRAWN BY E. N

of New Bedford

The Forbes Lith M'f'g Co Boston

BRITISH SHIP GEORGETTE.

NEW BEDFORD.

LL,

JOHN J. BRESLIN, CHIEF OF THE RESCUING PARTY.

Escape

John T Richardson was an American closely involved in Australia's most extraordinary prison break. A whaling ship agent in the port of New Bedford, Massachusetts, he was approached in 1875 by members of Clan na Gael, an Irish revolutionary organisation, to help them buy a ship and appoint a captain to undertake a voyage to Western Australia. But this was to be no ordinary money-making trip. The secret aim was to rescue six imprisoned Irish rebels – members of the Fenian Brotherhood, who had staged an unsuccessful rebellion in Ireland in 1867 – from Fremantle Prison.

Richardson's son-in-law, Captain George S Anthony, had quit the sea for a job in the Morse Twist Drill Works. Restless there, he approached Richardson for a ship only to be told that he had 'something better'. Anthony was introduced to John Devoy of Clan na Gael, who offered him a ship and the excitement of a daring rescue. It must have been a difficult moment for Anthony: he was only recently married with a baby daughter, his mother was ill and capture would have meant years in prison far from America. But Devoy and others are thought to have awoken in him a 'personal interest in the men [the Fenians] whose zeal for patriotism had placed them in an unfortunate position'.

Anthony took the job, and he and Richardson bought the whaling ship *Catalpa* for Clan na Gael. The ship was fitted out for a whaling voyage of 18 months and a mixed crew of Americans and so-called 'Malays' (South-East Asian seamen with names like Mopsy Roso and Zempa Malay) were hired. As the *Catalpa* set sail for Western Australia, flying from the masthead was the 'JTR' (John T Richardson) pennant of the ship's agent.

The same pennant was flying on 18 April 1876 as six Fenians clambered aboard the *Catalpa* off the Western Australian coast, south of Fremantle.

Picked up from Rockingham Beach, they had spent all night in an open whaleboat commanded by Anthony, having successfully avoided capture by the ships the colonial authorities had sent out to look for them. The pennant was most likely also flying on 24 August as the *Catalpa* put into New Bedford, where it was welcomed by a 70-gun salute and a crowd of thousands who swarmed over the vessel and 'carried away everything which was not too large for souvenirs'. The pennant survives in the care of Captain Anthony's descendants to this day.

(above and facing) **'Escape of Fenian convicts from West Australia'** 1876
Australian National Maritime Museum

(previous page) ***Bark* Catalpa *of New Bedford** 1876
by EN Russell
New Bedford Whaling Museum

The Kelly armour

Of all the scenes in Australian history none is more dramatic than that of a wounded iron-clad figure emerging out of the mist and advancing towards an inn besieged by police at Glenrowan, in northern Victoria. It was dawn on 28 June 1880, and outlaw Edward 'Ned' Kelly had come to rescue his brother, Dan, and fellow gang member, Steve Hart, who were trapped in the inn. Inside, another member of the gang, Joe Byrne, already lay dead, killed by police gunfire. All four men were wearing makeshift armour, manufactured secretly in the bush during the previous winter from the mould boards of ploughs.

As Ned Kelly lurched forward that morning, the sight unnerved his opponents. Artist Thomas Carrington saw something with 'no head visible', more like a ghost than a man, and with a 'very long thick neck'. Others described demons and devils, and railway guard Jesse Dowsett thought the man with the iron helmet looked 'nine feet' (2.7 metres) tall.

Constable George Arthur, however, simply saw some madman on the loose with a nail can on his head. He called out to Kelly that he would be shot if he kept moving, but the outlaw coolly swept back the folds of his oilskin coat and raised the revolver in his right hand. 'I could shoot you, sonny,' Kelly warned. With that, Arthur fired; the bullet struck Ned's helmet, forcing him back, but he recovered enough to fire.

For a while Kelly's armour protected him. Bleeding profusely from wounds received during the previous night's run-in with the police, he staggered under the armour's weight towards the inn, shouting to Steve and Dan, 'Come out, come out, boys, and we'll whip the beggars'. Called on to surrender, he yelled back his defiance: 'Never, while I've a shot left'. Eventually, with a despairing cry of 'I'm done,

I'm done', he was brought down by wounds to his unprotected legs, and captured alive.

After the siege at Glenrowan the police took away all four sets of armour. When a request came to have them displayed at the Beechworth Museum, Captain Frederick Standish, Commissioner of Police, was outraged. He proposed to the government that the suits be destroyed at once to prevent the growth of any 'Kelly-heroism'. But they have survived, and seen together they are a striking reminder of one of the most daring challenges to the forces of law and order in Australian history.

(previous page, left to right)

Armour worn by Ned Kelly 1879
State Library of Victoria

Armour worn by Joseph Byrne 1879
private collection

Armour worn by Dan Kelly 1879
Victoria Police Museum

Armour worn by Steve Hart 1879
Victoria Police Museum

(facing, clockwise from top left)

Ned Kelly on the day before he was hanged 10 November 1880
photograph by Charles Nettleton
University of Melbourne archives

Dan Kelly about 1877
Victoria Police Museum

Steve Hart 1877
Victoria Police Museum

Joe Byrne's body being photographed after the siege at Glenrowan 29 June 1880
State Library of Victoria

The Cross of Cong

One of the great moments of any ceremony in a Catholic cathedral comes when a cardinal, fully clothed in his red robes, processes to the altar with his attendant priests, amid swirls of incense. Australia's first cardinal was Irishman Patrick Francis Moran, appointed in 1885. Moran was determined to show Australian Catholics of Irish descent their cultural inheritance, the rich iconography of the early Christian church in Ireland. One of the objects he brought out from Ireland was a full-sized replica of the Cross of Cong, which was carried before him as he strode to the altar.

The original Cross of Cong, a twelfth-century Irish Christian processional cross, beautifully worked with Celtic designs in gold and silver, was made to house a relic of the cross of Christ. It was hidden away in the mid-seventeenth century, rediscovered in the nineteenth century and ended up in the National Museum of Ireland, where it is regarded as one of the museum's greatest treasures. A replica was made by Dublin jeweller Edmund Johnson for the Chicago World's Fair of 1893, and copies were made by Tiffany's of New York. Moran brought one of these fine replicas to Sydney, where it testified to the antiquity and splendour of Australia's Irish-dominated Catholic Church.

Replica of the Cross of Cong 1893
by Edmund Johnson
St Mary's Cathedral, Sydney

A model cathedral

Hailed at its official dedication and opening in October 1897 as the 'greatest ecclesiastical edifice in Australia', St Patrick's Cathedral, Melbourne, had already been on show to Victorians for years. The Melbourne International Exhibition of 1880 featured a plaster of Paris model of St Patrick's made by monumental mason James McGowan. After the exhibition closed in March 1881, McGowan presented it to the Catholic Church. The model showed donors to Archbishop Thomas Carr's cathedral fund what their money was helping to build.

In 1939 Archbishop Daniel Mannix oversaw the completion of the cathedral spires. That same year he gave McGowan's model to the Public Library and Museum of Victoria. Why give it away? Perhaps because the model reflected architect William Wardell's original ideas for the spires, and Mannix had ensured they were built to a height greater than originally planned. He wanted them to tower above the eastern end of the city, supposedly above the Parliament of Victoria. McGowan's model had become the vision of another time and so was relegated to a museum. Today, however, it has come back to St Patrick's, where it is displayed as a tribute to that generation of Irish Catholic immigrants, and their Australian children, who gave their shillings and pence to build it.

(previous page and above) **Model of St Patrick's Cathedral** 1880
by James McGowan
State Library of Victoria

Archbishop Mannix
Melbourne Diocesan Historical Commission of the Catholic
Archdiocese of Melbourne

An orrery from Ireland

It is difficult now to catch that tone of condescension, superiority, and often outright racism with which the Irish, especially the Catholic Irish, were once confronted in the Australian colonies. Jokes and cartoons ridiculing supposed Irish stupidity, illiteracy and general racial inferiority were commonplace in magazines such as the Sydney and Melbourne editions of *Punch*. So it is hardly surprising that the Catholic Irish worked hard to give their children an education that would allow them to get on – and move up – in colonial society. For their daughters, those who were better off turned to the Irish nuns. By the 1880s and 1890s, quality teaching and facilities could be found in such schools as Loreto College, Mary's Mount, Ballarat, Victoria.

The founder of the college, and its first principal, was Irishwoman Mother Mary Gonzaga Barry of the Institute of the Blessed Virgin Mary, better known as the Loreto Sisters. She had a simple message for her pupils: 'Set before yourself something which will ennoble your life, your thoughts and your endeavours. Aim at something excellent'.

For her day, Mother Barry had an extremely advanced approach to girls' education; the Loreto curriculum encompassed, among much else, literature, mathematics, languages, music, painting, science and history. The school even possessed an orrery, a mechanical model of the solar system, which they used to teach the basics of astronomy. This rare device – there were only three in Australia at the time – was sent out from Ireland by Mother Barry's brother.

Orrery used at Loreto College, Ballarat about 1900
Loreto Centre, Ballarat, Victoria

Kings in grass castles

Kings in Grass Castles (1959) and *Sons in the Saddle* (1983) were the books in which Mary Durack captured the saga of pastoral Australia. The Duracks and their relatives from the Tully, Costello and Kilfoyle families, were mostly poor Irish immigrants who arrived in the late 1840s and early 1850s. Their drive, initiative and family cohesiveness took them from small settlements around Goulburn to the Kimberleys in the far north-west of the continent, where they founded a pastoral empire.

The most prominent Duracks were Patrick ('Patsy'), who came to Australia in 1853, and his son, Michael Patrick or 'MP'. Patsy made a fortune and lost it in the great depression of the 1890s. MP, born in Australia, went into partnership with two Irishmen, Francis Connor and Dennis Doherty, and until his retirement in 1950, managed the vast Connor, Doherty and Durack properties

that stretched across the Western Australian and Northern Territory borders in the Kimberley.

Horses, cattle, river crossings, long stock drives, endless night camps under the stars and many wearisome hours in the saddle – this was the life of those Irish pastoral settlers and their European and Aboriginal drovers. Patsy Durack died in 1898, still mourning the death of his wife, Mary. At the end, he called out for her and his Aboriginal employee and friend, Pumpkin: 'Tell Pumpkin to fetch up the horses, Mary. I am ready now'.

Saddle from Newry station, a Connor, Doherty and Durack property 1930–50
Newry station, Northern Territory

Mary Durack (top left) with her father, Michael Patrick Durack, and her sister, Elizabeth, at Ivanhoe station, Western Australia about 1930
Battye Library, State Library of Western Australia

Tropical habit

On 6 June 1907 an amazing sight was to be seen at Beagle Bay, Dampier Peninsula, Western Australia. Wading ashore, through water over a metre deep, were six Irish nuns, Sisters of St John of God, in black habits. In wet clothes and bare feet they walked 11 kilometres to their new home, the Pallottine Fathers' mission station. The sisters were part of a party of nine led by Mother Antonio O'Brien; seven came from the order's mother house in County Wexford, Ireland, and two from Perth.

In their early years at Beagle Bay, and later in Broome, the St John of God sisters wore their characteristic long black habits. When Irishman Father John Creagh arrived in 1916, he was horrified at their living conditions. Among other improvements, Creagh ordered white bales of cotton from Perth, and the sisters gradually adopted lighter, white habits more suitable for work in the tropics.

The sisters today are working actively for reconciliation, having acknowledged that in the past they were one of those agents of change that had a destructive effect on the culture and society of Indigenous Australians in the north-west. Many of that 'stolen generation' of children, educated by the nuns and boarded in their institutions, have spoken favourably of the Irish sisters, recalling how they genuinely seemed to care about them. Not long before she died in 2007, after 67 years at Beagle Bay, Sister Bernadette O'Connor was asked whether she wanted to go home to Ireland. 'Why should I want to do that?' she replied. 'You are my people.'

Tropical habit for the Sisters of St John of God
St John of God Heritage Centre, Perth

John Wayland, Irish piper

John Shaw Wayland died, forgotten, at Nazareth House Nursing Home, Geraldton, Western Australia, in May 1954. Once he had been the toast of the town: during the First World War, he would play his pipes as he escorted local recruits for the Australian Imperial Force to the station. The townspeople gave him a little medal for that.

Wayland was born in Ireland in 1868, the year the last convict ship, carrying Irish Fenian rebels, went from Britain to Western Australia. By the late 1890s Wayland was one of Ireland's best known traditional pipers, playing the Irish or uillean pipes, and a founder of the Cork Pipers Club. In 1912 he came to Perth, bringing with him a set of rare uillean pipes. For many years his playing was a feature of events such as St Patrick's Day, first in Perth and later in Geraldton, where he settled. On Anzac Day 1938 Geraldton residents were moved when they heard Wayland play the old lament, 'The flowers of the forest'. Perhaps he had seen again some of those young faces of men he had accompanied to the station but who never returned home.

John Wayland 1911
Dease Studio, Perth
courtesy Ormonde Waters Jnr

POBLACHT NA H EIREANN.

THE PROVISIONAL GOVERNMENT
OF THE
IRISH REPUBLIC
TO THE PEOPLE OF IRELAND.

IRISHMEN AND IRISHWOMEN : In the name of God and of the dead generations from which she receives her old tradition of nationhood, Ireland, through us, summons her children to her flag and strikes for her freedom.

Having organised and trained her manhood through her secret revolutionary organisation, the Irish Republican Brotherhood, and through her open military organisations, the Irish Volunteers and the Irish Citizen Army, having patiently perfected her discipline, having resolutely waited for the right moment to reveal itself, she now seizes that moment, and, supported by her exiled children in America and by gallant allies in Europe, but relying in the first on her own strength, she strikes in full confidence of victory.

We declare the right of the people of Ireland to the ownership of Ireland, and to the unfettered control of Irish destinies, to be sovereign and indefeasible. The long usurpation of that right by a foreign people and government has not extinguished the right, nor can it ever be extinguished except by the destruction of the Irish people. In every generation the Irish people have asserted their right to national freedom and sovereignty ; six times during the past three hundred years they have asserted it in arms. Standing on that fundamental right and again asserting it in arms in the face of the world, we hereby proclaim the Irish Republic as a Sovereign Independent State, and we pledge our lives and the lives of our comrades-in-arms to the cause of its freedom, of its welfare, and of its exaltation among the nations.

The Irish Republic is entitled to, and hereby claims, the allegiance of every Irishman and Irishwoman. The Republic guarantees religious and civil liberty, equal rights and equal opportunities to all its citizens, and declares its resolve to pursue the happiness and prosperity of the whole nation and of all its parts, cherishing all the children of the nation equally, and oblivious of the differences carefully fostered by an alien government, which have divided a minority from the majority in the past.

Until our arms have brought the opportune moment for the establishment of a permanent National Government, representative of the whole people of Ireland and elected by the suffrages of all her men and women, the Provisional Government, hereby constituted, will administer the civil and military affairs of the Republic in trust for the people.

We place the cause of the Irish Republic under the protection of the Most High God, Whose blessing we invoke upon our arms, and we pray that no one who serves that cause will dishonour it by cowardice, inhumanity, or rapine. In this supreme hour the Irish nation must, by its valour and discipline and by the readiness of its children to sacrifice themselves for the common good, prove itself worthy of the august destiny to which it is called.

Signed on Behalf of the Provisional Government,

THOMAS J. CLARKE.

SEAN Mac DIARMADA.   THOMAS MacDONAGH.
P. H. PEARSE,   EAMONN CEANNT,
JAM CONNOLLY.   JOSEPH PLUNKETT.

Irish nationalism

Declarations of independence are dramatic events in any nation's history. On Easter Monday 1916, Commandant-General Pádraic Pearse of the Army of the Irish Republic, on behalf of the Provisional Government of the Irish Republic, stepped outside the General Post Office in the heart of Dublin and read a proclamation calling the republic into existence: 'Ireland, through us, summons her children to her flag and strikes for her freedom'.

This act marked the start of the famous Easter Rising. For just over a week, rebel forces held out in various locations throughout the city, but the end was inevitable. The United Kingdom of Great Britain and Ireland was at war, and 16 of the rebel leaders were executed after they surrendered. Most Irish, and Irish communities throughout the world, condemned the rebellion. The executions, however, sparked sympathy for the rebels and criticism of Britain.

The rebellion and its fate would come to have a profound effect on politics back in Australia. In the second half of 1916, the nation became involved in an often bitter campaign to introduce compulsory conscription for overseas military service. Until then, recruitment had been voluntary, but the large losses of men in France convinced Prime Minister William Morris Hughes that conscription was essential. However, in two referendums, held in October 1916 and December 1917, the Australian people narrowly rejected conscription.

Opposing Hughes over conscription was the Irish Archbishop of Melbourne, Daniel Mannix. After the Easter Rising Mannix increasingly took up the cause of an Irish republic, and in Australia he became one of the most prominent anti-conscription leaders. Hughes accused Mannix and others who opposed him of being virtual traitors to Australia and to the Empire in its hour of need. Mannix fought back

by declaring that Catholics were loyal to Australia, but that did not mean they automatically accepted British rule in Ireland.

The level of division and bitterness in the Australian community was one rarely experienced before or since. St Patrick's Day processions in Melbourne, led by Mannix, took on the appearance of Irish national demonstrations with floats depicting the 'martyrs of 1916'. In March 1918 it became an offence to advocate the independence of Ireland and a number of Irish Australians were imprisoned.

The uproar died away after a treaty was signed between Irish and British leaders in December 1921; it gave Ireland independence within the British Empire, but withheld republican status. For his part, Mannix remained the Australian champion of complete Irish republican independence for the rest of his long life.

Proclamation of the Irish Republic 1916
National Museum of Ireland

In loving memory

On 24 May 1917, in a room in a hospital in Memphis, Tennessee, Australian boxing champion, Les Darcy, aged 21, died from pneumonia contracted after a bout of septicaemia. At Darcy's bedside that day was his sweetheart, Winnie O'Sullivan, who cut off a small piece of Darcy's hair that she kept, along with her favourite photo of him, in a small golden locket. When O'Sullivan died in 1974, the locket was discovered among her possessions; her family had been unaware of its existence.

It later came to light that O'Sullivan's brother, Maurice, a great mate of Les Darcy, carried the locket at the end of his watch chain for many years and would show it to anyone who asked.

Of Irish Catholic descent, and a faithful Catholic himself, Les Darcy rose to boxing fame in the early years of the First World War. This success allowed him to build a house for his mother and to assist his poor family. In the heated atmosphere of Australia's conscription debates in 1916, Darcy slipped secretly away to America where he intended to make enough money from his boxing career to ensure his parents could live comfortably, and then to enlist for war service. Many in Australia, some in high places, accused him of cowardice, and in America he was unable to obtain fights that paid him well.

When Darcy's body was returned to Australia he was given a hero's funeral. He was adopted by the Catholic community who saw him as unjustly persecuted, as he had only wished to help his family, and then do his duty for his country.

Locket belonging to Winnie O'Sullivan 1917
National Museum of Australia

Winnie O'Sullivan 1912
National Museum of Australia

Two monstrances

In the Catholic church a monstrance is a most religious and highly significant vessel. It is used to display to the faithful a piece of consecrated bread, known as the Blessed Sacrament, which Catholics believe has become the real body of Christ during the mass. On special feast days, such as Corpus Christi (Body of Christ), a large and highly decorated monstrance might be used to carry the Blessed Sacrament in procession around the parish. Betty Dolan of the Parish of St Augustine's, Coolangatta, Queensland, remembers Corpus Christi in the 1940s and 1950s being attended by the Brisbane diocese's Irish-born archbishop, James Duhig: 'Parishioners, sodality members, and visitors would assemble in procession from the church on McLean Street, led by cross bearer Keith Farrell and the clergy, [and] Archbishop Duhig … carrying the monstrance under a canopy'.

A far more modest monstrance than that carried by Archbishop Duhig was in occasional use in the 1920s and 1930s in O'Shea's Railway Hotel in Katherine in the Northern Territory. Tim O'Shea came to Australia in 1900 and acquired mining and bush skills in northern Queensland. In 1907 he returned to Ireland to marry Catherine O'Keeffe. The couple returned to Australia and settled in the Northern Territory. O'Shea worked as a prospector, blacksmith and, finally, owner of pubs including the one at Katherine and Tattersall's Hotel at Borroloola. Good Catholics, the O'Sheas had mass said in their hotel by visiting priests, and their simple family monstrance is a relic of those days, still treasured by their descendants.

(above and previous page) **Monstrance belonging to O'Shea family** 1928
on loan from Peter and Maureen Dunham

(previous page and facing) **Monstrance made from jewellery donated by Brisbane Catholics for the Cathedral of the Holy Name** 1928
St Stephen's Cathedral, Brisbane

PRESENTED BY
LITTLE COMPANY OF MARY
Nᵀᴴ ADELAIDE.
TO
Most Reb. R.W. Spence. O.P. D.D.
Archbishop of Adelaide
ON LAYING FOUNDATION STONE
HOSPITAL EAST WING.
1ˢᵗ July, 1917.

Spence the Builder

Australian Catholics were used to opening their wallets to help their church. Over the decades they donated a sizeable sum towards the building of churches, presbyteries, church halls, catholic schools, convents and monasteries. Such buildings are dotted across Australia, from city centres to suburbs, country towns and smaller rural settlements, and constitute the most visible legacy of the Irish Catholic presence.

South Australia was always regarded as the least Irish and Catholic of the Australian colonies. Nevertheless, during the reign of Irishman Robert William Spence as Catholic archbishop of Adelaide (1915–34), his diocese experienced a veritable building boom. Spence officiated at the laying of foundation stones, and the opening of more than 85 major church buildings. The man who became known as 'Spence the Builder' was proud of this

achievement because, as he saw it, thousands of ordinary Catholics had contributed to the expansion of their church. Spence had the many silver trowels he used on these occasions mounted onto shields for display at his official residence.

Ceremonial building trowels presented to Archbishop Spence
1914–40
Archives and Records Services, Catholic Archdiocese of Adelaide

>CHIF'S CHAIR<
THE CHAIR USED BY THE LATE
PRIME MINISTER of AUSTRALIA
BEN CHIFLEY
WHEN HE ATTENDED MASS
at St. Christopher's Church

Chif's chair

The Catholic church has traditionally disapproved of marriages between Catholics and non-Catholics. In 1908 the Pope announced the famous 'Ne Temere' decree, which ruled all marriages between Catholics and others invalid unless conducted by a Catholic priest.

This decree affected the relationship between Ben Chifley and Elizabeth McKenzie of Bathurst, New South Wales. Chifley was Irish Catholic on all sides of his family, and McKenzie was a Presbyterian with Scottish parents, who were definitely not in favour of her converting to Catholicism in order to marry Chifley. And so, in June 1914, they married in a Presbyterian church, Chifley taking the view that 'one of us has to take the knock. It had better be me'. The 'knock' for him meant that for having married outside his church he was barred from taking communion, and the church did not regard his marriage as legitimate, even though it was legal.

The Chifleys would simply have been another couple whose lives were complicated by a mixed marriage but for the fact that theirs were lived in the spotlight of public attention. Chifley was a leading Labor politician and, on Prime Minister John Curtin's death in 1945, he became prime minister of Australia. He never deserted his church. When in Canberra, he often attended mass at St Christopher's Cathedral, where he sat in the back of the church on what is now preserved there as 'Chif's chair'.

Ben and Elizabeth Chifley 1940s
Bathurst Historical Society, New South Wales

Chair used by Prime Minister Ben Chifley in church 1940s
St Christopher's Cathedral, Canberra

Sister Brenda Browne and the '49ers'

County Kerry people remember their own. On
5 July 2010 Kerry Radio reported the passing of
centenarian Sister Brenda Browne, of Brisbane,
Australia. A Sister of Mercy, she was originally
Mary 'Bidge' Browne from Ballyhorgan, Ballyduff,
County Kerry, who left Ireland for Australia in
1924, aged 19. There she spent the rest of her long
life serving the order by teaching in Queensland
Catholic schools.

Sister Brenda did not come to Queensland alone.
She was part of a group of 49 young novices from
Ireland, all offering their lives to the service of God.
The order looked to Ireland as a source of dedicated
teachers, nurses and social workers, and the '49ers',
as they were known, were just one of many groups
who came to Brisbane in the 1920s and 1930s.

In an age before jet travel, few of these young
novices expected to see Ireland, or their families,
again. Leaving Ireland in 1947, Sister Angela Doyle,
also bound for Brisbane, wrote: 'We did not dwell
too long on the sacrifice that this entailed. We were
giving our lives to God and we would do it willingly
and as cheerfully as the pain of parting allowed …
As we sailed further from our homeland, we put
our faith and trust in God for the future'.

Sister Brenda Browne, aged 103 2008
Brisbane Sisters of Mercy, Congregation Archives

(previous page and facing) The '49ers', Tamborine,
Queensland (Sister Brenda Browne is third from left,
third row from front) about 1924
photograph by Father Francis Browne
The Father Browne SJ Collection

Searching for Ireland

Australian poet and academic Vincent Buckley was born in 1925 in a cottage behind his uncle's pub, in a region north of Melbourne much settled by the Irish in the mid-nineteenth century. He described his Condon, Scanlan and Buckley ancestors as being 'typical' and 'anonymous', their sense of being Irish having been lost in becoming Australian. This, Buckley believed, was contrary to popular belief that saw Catholics in Australia as having preserved a strong awareness of their Irish origins.

Perhaps it was this sense of disconnectedness with his Irish past that led Buckley into an ever-deepening search for that part of him that was 'Irish'. His frequent visits to the country naturally took him to sites such as the ancient tower in County Galway associated with William Butler Yeats, Ireland's most famous twentieth-century poet. Yeats also struggled with what it meant to be Irish, but Buckley seems to have become somewhat disillusioned with the Ireland of the 1970s. Interestingly, in one of his last published poems, he circles back pensively to his Australian birthplace, Romsey:

> I see Romsey through a hole in the wind,
> as I used to in late autumn, in the southern gales …
> I smell the printer's ink, and books,
> and dust that flashes when the raindrops hit it
> as it takes the rain into itself.

Vincent Buckley at Yeats Tower, Gort, Ireland 1973
courtesy Penelope Buckley

That's my language

In mid-June 1975 a man driving down Parramatta Road in Sydney suddenly stopped in the middle of the traffic, got out and started to dance. 'That's my language, that's my music,' he shouted. He had tuned in to the Turkish program of Australia's first ethnic radio station, 2EA. Irishwoman Claire Dunne, foundation director of 2EA Sydney and 3EA Melbourne, would recall how Arabic speakers cried to hear the sounds of their own country over the air. Soon program coordinators were telling her that people from different ethnic groups were writing in to say there was now no need to return to their homeland – 'Home is Australia'.

Dunne's support for multicultural Australia arose out of her own strong sense of her Irish heritage. Revisiting Ireland, and reconnecting with Irish music, brought Dunne back to Australia with a growing awareness that it was this music that

most strongly expressed Irish cultural identity. Immigrants, she realised, needed to 'keep contact with what was foreign to Australia', for if they lost that, 'they lost part of themselves'. In 1999 Dunne was awarded the Medal of the Order of Australia for 'service to multiculturalism, particularly through the promotion of Celtic culture, and to ethnic broadcasting'.

3EA T-shirt 1970s
on loan from Claire Dunne

Claire Dunne
courtesy Claire Dunne

John Moriarty's fishing rod

Top sportsman, activist for Indigenous rights, federal public servant, designer and successful businessman – John Moriarty has been all of these. Like many Indigenous Australians he has an Irish surname, indicating his family links with that country. Moriarty was also one of the 'stolen generation', taken away from his Yanyuwa mother in the Northern Territory when he was four, and brought up in homes and schools in southern Australia.

John Moriarty's search for the Irish part of his identity took him to County Kerry in 1980, and to a meeting with Pat 'Aeroplane' O'Shea. O'Shea, aged 92, had been a star Gaelic footballer for Kerry before the First World War. After a 20-minute conversation with Moriarty in the doorway, O'Shea asked him in. He told him about a visit by Moriarty's father in 1928, even remembering how many trout they had caught when they went fishing together. From the back of a cupboard, O'Shea retrieved an old fishing rod, tied together in three pieces, and a separate brass reel. Apologising for the fact that the line had rotted away, he handed the rod to Moriarty with these words: 'He left it here for you'.

During his visit to Kerry, Moriarty met many of his Irish relatives for the first time, and found himself readily accepted by them. When 'Aeroplane' O'Shea died, a local paper recalled Moriarty's visit, confiding how the old family fishing rod was now 'safe in the hands of the Moriarty clan of Australia'.

(above and previous page) **Fishing rod and reel belonging to John Moriarty's father** 1928
on loan from John Moriarty

John Moriarty as a small child with his mother, Kathleen 1940s
National Museum of Australia

A contempt of oppressors

Father Ted Kennedy was proud of his Irish heritage. He called his hideaway house at Burrawang, in the Southern Highlands of New South Wales, 'Lisdoonvarna', after the parish in County Clare, Ireland, where his mother's people came from. Father Ted learnt his prayers, and his love of Irish stories and poetry, from his grandmother, Mary Jane McMahon, the widow of a Sydney publican. And describing him at his funeral in May 2005, the master of ceremonies, Danny Gilbert, drew on the words of Pádraic Pearse, the leader of Ireland's 1916 Easter Rising: 'Splendid and holy causes are served by splendid and holy men'.

The cause Father Ted served was that of bringing an intensely practical form of Christianity to the Catholic parish of Redfern he served between 1971 and 2005. Redfern's poor and marginalised, especially the Indigenous population, were encouraged to see the parish church of St Vincent's as very much their own, and his presbytery as a place all could turn to for help and encouragement. Father Ted, with co-workers like Aboriginal activist, Mum Shirl, worked tirelessly for justice and civil rights for Indigenous Australians. He lived by the lines from one of his favourite poems, Ezra Pound's 'Commission':

> *Bear my contempt of oppressors.*
> *Speak against unconscious oppression …*
> *Speak against bonds.*

Father Ted Kennedy of St Mary's, Redfern, with 14-month-old Duane Captain 1996
photograph by Palani Mohan, *Sydney Morning Herald*
Fairfaxphotos

The Irish raider

When he was growing up in Ireland, horse trainer Dermot Weld was given a book of Banjo Paterson's poems. They enthralled him, and within weeks he had memorised many of them: 'I visualised myself riding the ranges of that open country, rounding up cattle, herding sheep and experiencing heat'. Years later, Weld astonished a group of Australian journalists who had asked him whether he could recite any of Paterson's poems that were not about racing by launching into 'A bush christening':

> *On the outer Barcoo where the churches are few,*
> *And men of religion are scanty,*
> *On a road never cross'd 'cept by folk that are lost,*
> *One Michael Magee had a shanty.*

On that occasion, at Flemington racecourse on Tuesday 2 November 1993, Weld could afford to indulge his love of Paterson. He was celebrating having just become the trainer of the first overseas-trained horse to take out Australia's richest and most prestigious race – the Melbourne Cup.

Vintage Crop, trained by Weld in Ireland and owned by Sir Michael Smurfit, ran a great Melbourne Cup in 1993. In the last furlongs, the 'Irish raider', as he was dubbed, unleashed a magnificent run from the field to outpace the leaders. Weld had dreamt of taking out the Cup ever since his first reading of 'The Man from Snowy River', and now, like the 'colt from old Regret', the Melbourne Cup had 'got away' – to Ireland.

Vintage Crop passing the winning post in the Melbourne Cup 1993
photograph by Bruno Cannatelli
Ultimate Racing Photos

Roses of Tralee

In Ireland there is one television event that is right up there with the major sports finals – the annual Rose of Tralee festival. In August 2010 it rated as the most watched show of the year on any television channel available in Ireland. Since its inception in the late 1950s, the 'Rose' has had its share of critics, but hosted for over 20 years by Ireland's most famous television and radio personality, Gay Byrne, the festival has always held centrestage in Ireland. Byrne sees it as a personality show in which the young female contestants might be anyone's daughter, sister or niece. By allowing any young woman of Irish descent worldwide to enter, the festival reaches out like nothing else in Ireland to the huge Irish diaspora in countries like Australia.

To date, three Australians have been crowned the Rose of Tralee: Nyomi Horgan, 1995; Lisa Manning, 2001; and Kathryn Anne Feeney, 2006.

All three women have stressed how participating in the competition, and winning the title, has helped them to reconnect strongly with their Irish origins. Nyomi Horgan says that she discovered 'resemblances that have survived the generations' and enjoys the 'bond that makes us family'.

Kathryn Feeney 2006
Rose of Tralee International Festival

Rose of Tralee winner's crown 2006
on loan from Kathryn Feeney

The 'Irish experiment'

The Australian Football League's so-called 'Irish experiment' began in 1982, when the Melbourne Football Club's legendary coach, Ron Barassi, travelled to Ireland to watch some Gaelic football. Barassi believed that the two games had many similarities, and that the Irish game could offer a source of untapped talent for the league.

One Irishman attracted to Australia by Barassi was Jimmy Stynes. And an exceptional recruit he proved to be. In 1991 Stynes became the league's first and only overseas player to be awarded the prestigious Brownlow Medal for the season's 'fairest and best'. An official 'legend' of the Melbourne Football Club, Stynes competed in 244 consecutive games. After he left football in 1998, he took on the cause of Indigenous players as the AFL's anti-racism officer, and today is well known for his work with young people through the Reach Foundation that continues despite his high-profile battle with cancer.

Another successful Irish recruit is Tadhg Kennelly. Playing for the winning Sydney Swans in the 2005 AFL Grand Final, Kennelly famously danced an Irish jig for the television cameras after the match. Returning to Ireland after the death of his father, he played in the County Kerry team that won the 2009 All Ireland (Gaelic) Football Final, so completing a unique double. He danced a little jig on that occasion also.

Tadhg Kennelly dances a jig on the podium after Kerry's All Ireland Football Final win over Cork 2009
photograph by Brendan Moran
Sportsfile

Jimmy Stynes takes a mark, AFL Round 8 match, 1998, Melbourne versus Collingwood
GSP Images, Slattery Media Group

object list

In the search for material for this exhibition, curators from the National Museum of Australia travelled far and wide. They met with managers in great national institutions, local collectors in small museums and individuals in their homes. These people freely gave their time and shared the stories that belong to their objects. This list represents their willingness to entrust their treasures to the care of the Museum to tell the story of the Irish in Australia.

Arriving

Transportation

***Rajah* quilt** 1841
made by female convicts during their
journey to Australia on the *Rajah*
National Gallery of Australia

***Charlotte* medal** 1788
attributed to Thomas Barrett
Australian National Maritime Museum

Journal of a Voyage to New South Wales
1790
by John White
published by J Debrett, London
National Library of Australia

Replica cat-o-nine tails 1900s
National Museum of Australia

**Indent (list of convicts) sent aboard
the transport ship *Queen*** April 1791
State Records of New South Wales

A Voyage to New South Wales **(Russian
version)** 1803
State Library of New South Wales

Wax portrait of George Barrington
about 1790
National Museum of Australia

**Medal for outstanding achievement
awarded to Henry Halloran** 1824
made by Samuel Clayton
on loan from Les Carlisle

**Medal for outstanding achievement
awarded to Charles Driver** 1823
made by Samuel Clayton
Powerhouse Museum, Sydney, gift of Bob
Edmunds, 1988

**Medal for outstanding achievement
awarded to JF Josephson** 1826
made by Samuel Clayton
private collection

Bushranger Martin Cash's walking stick gun 1840s
Tasmanian Museum and Art Gallery

Bushranger Martin Cash's powder flask 1840s
State Library of Tasmania

Thomas Greer's petition 1838
State Records of New South Wales

Headstone for Thomas Greer's grave 1841
Berry and District Historical Society

Dennis Dogherty, Port Arthur 1874
National Library of Australia

Convict jacket about 1840s
National Museum of Australia

Leather side cap 1840s
National Museum of Australia

Leg irons 1850s
National Museum of Australia

John Mitchel's '82 Club' coat and sash
National Museums Northern Ireland

John Mitchel's pistol 1840s
National Museum of Ireland, Dublin

Sword presented to Thomas Francis Meagher in America 1860s
Waterford Museum of Treasures

Portrait drawing of Thomas Francis Meagher 1847
Waterford Museum of Treasures

The William Smith O'Brien Gold Cup 1854
National Museum of Ireland, Dublin

Immigration

The anchor of the *Nashwauk* 1855
City of Onkaparinga, South Australia

'Articles recommended by the Destitute Board to be supplied to the wrecked immigrants ex "Nashwauk"' 1855
State Records of South Australia

Female emigration poster, Cork 1836
State Library of New South Wales

Father Dixon's crucifix about 1803
Sydney Archdiocesan Archives

Wooden tabernacle 1817
Sydney Archdiocesan Archives

Stained glass window from temporary Anglican church 1836
Holy Trinity Church, Adelaide

Mother-of-pearl cross brought to Australia from Argentina late 19th century
Sisters of Mercy, Perth, Western Australia

Emu egg clock belonging to Mother Vincent Whitty 1871
Mercy International Centre, Dublin, Ireland

Hourglass used for timing daily prayers 1830s
Sisters of Charity, Sydney

Piece of peat brought from Ireland about 1875
Loreto Centre, Ballarat, Victoria

Illuminated commemorative manuscript dedicated to Sister Clara Mary Frayne 1857
Sisters of Mercy, Victoria

Brooch and earrings belonging to Mary (Hyndman) Smythe about 1880s
on loan from Anne Colville

Settle carved by Mary Hyndman 1908
on loan from Anne Colville

Grace McCrohan's prayer book 1830s
on loan from Peggy Darst Townsdin

Printed letter to Lord Monteagle from Patrick Danaher, Melbourne, Port Philip 1848
National Library of Ireland

Indoor register, Armagh Union workhouse 1847–48
Public Record Office of Northern Ireland

Pencil drawing of shipboard life on the *Thomas Arbuthnot* 1849
National Museum of Australia

Sea chest belonging to Margaret Hurley, Gort workhouse, County Galway 1849
on loan from the Perry family

Female immigrant bonnet 1860s
Historic Houses Trust of New South Wales

Mary Kineily's Female Servant's Agreement 1864
State Records of New South Wales

An Emigrant Ship, Dublin Bay, Sunset 1853
by Edwin Hayes
National Gallery of Ireland, Dublin

Model of immigrant ship *Inconstant*
Museum of Wellington and the Sea

Settling

Agriculture and pastoralism

The Durack Women 1988
by Sheila Stump, Rowena Branch, Country Women's Association of New South Wales
National Museum of Australia

Aboriginal shield from Bulloo River area given to Francis and Anne Tully 1911
National Museum of Australia

Connor and Doherty saddle 1930–50
Newry station, Northern Territory

Kilfoyle branding irons, Rosewood Station 1890s–1930s
private loan

Compass used on the Kimberley expedition led by Stumpy Durack 1882
Western Australian Museum

Kings in Grass Castles [1959] 1985
by Mary Durack
published by Constable, London
on loan from Richard Reid

Laundry table, Murndal 1850s
private collection

Travelling library trunk and rare books belonging to Samuel Pratt Winter
private collection

Antlers of extinct Irish elk
private collection

Murndal wool bale stencil
private collection

Needle for stitching potato bags, potato bag, potato knife and digging fork from Koroit
on loan from Mary Kelly

Milk churn, butter pat and butter stamp about 1880s
Kangaroo Valley Historical Society, New South Wales

Patrick Devery's cow bell 1850
Gerringong Heritage Centre

Kiama Agricultural Society's 'List of prizes' 1855
University of Wollongong Library/ Archive, Frank McCaffrey Collection (on loan from the Weston family, Kiama)

John King's prize cup won for his 'Champion Keg of Butter' 1891
Kangaroo Valley Historical Society

Exploration and rural settlement

Robert O'Hara Burke's pistol 1860
State Library of Victoria

Memorandum of the Start of the Exploring Expedition 1860
by Nicholas Chevalier
Art Gallery of South Australia

Yandruwandha Aboriginal breastplate 1861
South Australian Museum

Map created for Victorian parliament to show land available for selection 1862
Public Record Office Victoria

Sir John O'Shanassy, Premier of Victoria 1881
by Marshall Wood
State Library of Victoria, Melbourne

Father John Joseph Therry's clerical collar and chalice 1820s
Sydney Archdiocesan Archives

Father Therry's marriage dollar 1803
St Mary's Cathedral, Archdiocese of Sydney

Note to Father John Joseph Therry 1820s
State Library of New South Wales

Contact

Leangle (hooked) club 1836
National Museums Northern Ireland

Flattened, bi-conical head-shaped club 1836
National Museums Northern Ireland

Decorated shields 1836
National Museums Northern Ireland

Curved hunting and fighting boomerang with tapering ends 1836
National Museums Northern Ireland

Rectangular-shaped basket of split cane 1836
National Museums Northern Ireland

Ceremonial emu feather girdle 1836
National Museums Northern Ireland

Fighting pick with metal blade collected by Francis Gillen 1890s
South Australian Museum

Francis Gillen's journal (Vol. II) 6 June – 7 August 1901
State Library of South Australia

Forehead band about 1890s
Gillen Collection, South Australian Museum

Necklet about 1890s
Gillen Collection, South Australian Museum

Address presented to Francis Gillen by fellow officers of the Overland Telegraph early 1900s
State Library of South Australia

Yawk Yawk X-ray style painting collected by Paddy Cahill early 1900s
Museum Victoria

Baldwin Spencer and Paddy Cahill 2006
by Gabriel Maralngurra
National Museum of Australia

Tropical habit worn by the Sisters of St John of God
Sisters of St John of God Heritage Centre, Perth

Violin used in the Bungarun Leprosarium orchestra about 1936
St John of God Heritage Centre, Old Convent, Broome

Gabardine suit worn by Daisy Bates about 1904–51
South Australian Museum

Leather satchel used by Daisy Bates about 1900–1935
Ayers House

Spearthrower collected by Daisy Bates from Aboriginal visitors to her Ooldea camp 1920s–1930s
National Museum of Australia

Cities

Doll's house and furniture about 1871
on loan from the Earl of Belmore

Upper Hunter Courier, **silk newspaper presented to the governor** 17 April 1871
on loan from the Earl of Belmore

Steamer *Agnes Irving with the Viceregal Cortege leaving Rocky Mouth for Grafton* 1869
by GH Bruhn
on loan from the Earl of Belmore

Levée uniform worn by Lord Belmore 1868–72
on loan from the Earl of Belmore

Somerset Richard Lowry-Corry, 4th Earl of Belmore (13th Governor of New South Wales) about 1873
by John Lucas
Historic Houses Trust of New South Wales, Government House, Sydney

Archaeological material from St Patrick's church, The Rocks excavated 1999
Sydney Foreshore Authority

St Patrick's St Vincent de Paul Conference, Poor Registers 1900–07
St Patrick's Parish Archives, Sydney

Building a new life

Power and politics

Cabinet portrait of Peter Lalor 1880s
Ballarat Fine Art Gallery

Pieces cut from the Eureka flag 1854
Ballarat Fine Art Gallery

Piece cut from the Eureka flag 1854
Gold Museum, Ballarat

Armour worn by Joseph Byrne 1879
private collection

Armour worn by Steve Hart 1879
Victoria Police Museum

Armour worn by Ned Kelly 1879
State Library of Victoria

Armour worn by Dan Kelly 1879
Victoria Police Museum

Scrapbook compiled by Constable Thomas McIntyre 1880
Victoria Police Museum

Black cap worn by Victorian Supreme Court Judges late 19th century
Supreme Court of Victoria

Court Book, Supreme Court, Victoria September–October 1880
Supreme Court of Victoria

Royal Irish Constabulary truncheon brought to Victoria about 1860
Victoria Police Museum

Scrapbook belonging to Constable Thomas Waldron
Victoria Police Museum

Booklet about Constable Thomas Waldron 1899
Victoria Police Museum

Testimonial presented to Superintendent William Brandish Montfort 1893
Victoria Police Museum

Insignia, Knight Grand Cross of the Order of St Michael and St George, presented to Sir John Madden 1906
Supreme Court of Victoria

Portrait of Sir John Madden, shown in the uniform of lieutenant governor of Victoria 1915
by L Murany
Supreme Court of Victoria

Portrait of William Charles Wentworth about 1850
by Richard Buckner
Legislative Assembly, Parliament House, Sydney

William Charles Wentworth's official court dress about 1855
Historic Houses Trust of New South Wales

Pages from the women's suffrage petition, including the front page and page with Mary Lee's signature 1894
South Australian Parliament

Irish nationalism

Marble sample board of Irish rocks made by Morgan Jageurs early 1890s
private collection

Táin Bó Cúailnge
O'Donnell Irish Collection, Academic Centre, Newman College and St Mary's College, University of Melbourne

Michael Dwyer's blunderbuss 1798
National Museum of Ireland, Dublin

Pike used in 1798 rebellion in Ireland 1798
Newtownabbey Borough Council, Northern Ireland

The Search for Michael Dwyer about 1810
by William Sadler II
National Gallery of Ireland, Dublin

JTR pennant from the *Catalpa* 1876
private collection

Pipe and chronometer belonging to Captain Anthony of the *Catalpa* 1870s

Navigational instruments and ship's box from the *Catalpa* 1876
private collection

Portrait of Captain Anthony about 1876
private collection

Joseph Graham O'Connor's scrapbook
National Library of Australia

The Monster Meeting of the 20th Sep 1843, at Clifden in the Irish Highlands
by Joseph Patrick Haverty
National Gallery of Ireland, Dublin

Daniel O'Connell commemorative medal 1847
National Museum of Ireland, Dublin

Certificate of membership of the Loyal Australasian Repeal Association 1844
Sydney Archdiocesan Archives

Original stained glass doors from Queensland Irish Association about 1900
Queensland Irish Association, Brisbane

Orange Lodge membership certificate issued to Thomas Wilson 24 April 1885
Gatton Historical Society, Gatton, Queensland

Alec Gall's Orange Lodge sash about 1880
Berry Historical Society, Berry, New South Wales

National President's collar, Hibernian-Australasian Catholic Benefit Society 1930s
National Museum of Australia

Processional banner used by the Hibernian-Australasian Catholic Benefit Society at St Patrick's Day celebrations 1930s
National Museum of Australia

Dispensation from the Hibernian-Australasian Catholic Benefit Society granted to members in Albury, enabling them to set up their own branch 1872
National Museum of Australia

Proclamation of the Irish Republic 1916
National Museum of Ireland, Dublin

Engraved silver casket that held the Freedom of Dublin, presented to Archbishop Mannix 1925
Melbourne Diocesan Historical Commission of the Catholic Archdiocese of Melbourne

Monstrance, a replica of the Cross of Cong, presented to Archbishop Daniel Mannix 1962
St Patrick's Cathedral, Melbourne

Clothing belonging to Archbishop Mannix
Melbourne Diocesan Historical
Commission of the Catholic Archdiocese
of Melbourne

William Joseph Fegan's diary, Darlinghurst Gaol 27 August 1918
private collection

Photograph of William Joseph Fegan, and fellow Irish Rebels internees, in Darlinghurst Gaol 1918
private collection

Religion

Model of St Patrick's Cathedral, Melbourne 1880s
by James McGowan
State Library of Victoria

Bound illuminated addresses presented to Archbishop Thomas Carr 1883–1901
Melbourne Diocesan Historical
Commission of the Catholic Archdiocese
of Melbourne

Vestments and mitre belonging to Archbishop Carr about 1895
Melbourne Diocesan Historical
Commission of the Catholic Archdiocese
of Melbourne

Replica of the Cashel Crozier belonging to Archbishop Daniel Mannix about 1895
St Patrick's Cathedral, Melbourne

Portrait in oils of Cardinal Patrick Francis Moran
by George de Pyroy
St Mary's Cathedral, Sydney

Cameo ring, with head of the Blessed Virgin, belonging to Cardinal Moran late 19th century
St Mary's Cathedral, Sydney

Pectoral cross belonging to Cardinal Moran late 19th century
made by JM Dempster
St Mary's Cathedral, Sydney

Replica of the Cross of Cong 1893
made by Edmund Johnson, Dublin
Archdiocese of Sydney and St Mary's
Cathedral, Sydney

Belleek shamrock pattern tea set
19th century
Sisters of Mercy, Parramatta, New South
Wales

Prie dieu, **used by Sisters of Mercy novices in Singleton, New South Wales, to take their vows**
Sisters of Mercy, Singleton, New South
Wales

Rings of deceased Sisters of Mercy
various dates
Sisters of Mercy, Singleton, New South
Wales

'The novice's guide', written by Mother Mary Stanislaus Kenny
1880s
Sisters of Mercy, Singleton, New South
Wales

Portrait of Mother Catherine McCauley after 1841
Sisters of Mercy, Melbourne
Congregation, Victoria

Chair used by Prime Minister Ben Chifley in church 1940s
St Christopher's Cathedral, Canberra

The Presbyterian Cookery Book, **owned by Elizabeth Chifley** 1902
Bathurst Historical Society, New South
Wales

James Parker's Irish prayer book, First Communion rosette and medal 1916
on loan from Michael Parker

James Parker's rosary beads and scapulars
on loan from Michael Parker

James Parker's pilgrimage medal, inscribed 'I have prayed for you at Lough Derg'
on loan from Michael Parker

Travelling confessional and portable holy wafer maker
St Rose's Parish, Kapunda, South Australia

Travelling anointing kit, used by Father Bernard Gurry 1920s–1930s
St Rose's Parish, Kapunda, South Australia

Children of Mary banner
St Rose's Parish, Kapunda, South Australia

Children of Mary veil and cape and medallion
Sydney Archdiocesan Archives

Around the Boree Log and Other Verses 1921
by Father Patrick Hartigan ('John O'Brien')
published by Angus and Robertson,
Sydney
National Library of Australia

Sash, Australian Holy Catholic Guild of St Mary and St Joseph early 1900s
Sydney Archdiocesan Archives

Catechism of Christian Doctrine 1937
Sydney Archdiocesan Archives

Mitre belonging to Archbishop Spence
St Laurence's Dominican Priory, Adelaide

Ceremonial building trowels presented to Archbishop Spence 1914–40
Archives and Records Services, Catholic
Archdiocese of Adelaide

Monstrance made from jewellery donated by Brisbane Catholics for the proposed Cathedral of the Holy Name 1928
St Stephen's Cathedral, Brisbane

Soil brought from Ireland for the foundations of the proposed Cathedral of the Holy Name 1920s
Catholic Archdiocese of Brisbane Catholic
Archives

Archbishop of Brisbane Sir James Duhig's centenary ring and centenary cross 1959
St Stephen's Cathedral, Brisbane

Archbishop of Brisbane Sir James Duhig's Roman hat
Catholic Archdiocese of Brisbane Catholic
Archives

Education

Needlework sampler book produced in Kilrea Female School, County Derry, Ireland mid-19th century
Migration Museum, Adelaide

Sequel No II to the Second Book of Lessons for the Use of Schools 1866
National Library of Australia

James Hackett's exercise book, Christian Brothers, Adelaide 1890
Christian Brothers College, Adelaide

Third Book of Reading Lessons by the Christian Brothers 1897
Christian Brothers College, Adelaide

Leather straps formerly used for corporal punishment
Christian Brothers College, Adelaide

Gym equipment used at Christian Brothers College, Adelaide early 20th century
Christian Brothers College, Adelaide

The Riverview Challenge Cup for Senior Eights 1893
by John Priora
Saint Ignatius' College, Riverview, Sydney

Orrery used at Loreto College, Ballarat about 1900
Loreto Centre, Ballarat, Victoria

Pencil box used at Loreto College, Adelaide 1940s
Loreto College, Adelaide

School hat, Loreto College, Adelaide 1950s
Loreto College, Adelaide

Concert harp, made by Frederick Grosjean, London, used in the Academy of Mary Immaculate, Melbourne
Sisters of Mercy, Melbourne Congregation, Victoria

Stave blackboard drawing device 1900
Sisters of Mercy, Melbourne Congregation, Victoria

Medicine

Dr Richard Thomas Tracy's ovariotomy instruments mid-19th century
Royal Women's Hospital, Melbourne

Diorama of Sisters of Charity opening their first hospital, St Vincent's, Sydney 1857
St Vincent's Hospital Archives, Melbourne

Sister Angela Mary Doyle's Officer of the Order of Australia Medal 1994
Mater Hospital Archives, Brisbane

Sister Angela Mary Doyle's Queensland Business Leaders Hall of Fame award 2009
Mater Hospital Archives, Brisbane

Arts and culture

Ornate lorikeets (*Trichoglossus ornatus*), collected by Alfred Russell Wallace about 1857
Museum Victoria, Melbourne

Original drawing of stick insects for the *Prodromus of the Zoology of Victoria*
by Arthur Bartholomew
Museum Victoria, Melbourne

Mating pair of double-eyed fig-parrot specimens, named 'M'Coy's Perroquet' after Frederick McCoy 1875
Museum Victoria, Melbourne

Prodromus of the Palæontology of Victoria: or, The Figures and Descriptions of Victorian Organic Remains 1874
by Frederick McCoy
published by John Ferres, Government Printer, Melbourne
National Museum of Australia

Plaster cast of *Venus de Milo* from Sir Redmond Barry's collection 1850s
private collection

Illuminated address presented to Sir Redmond Barry by members of the bar 7 February 1876
La Trobe Picture Collection, State Library of Victoria

Industry and business

Model railway engine and track 1878
built by apprentices at the Phoenix Foundry, Ballarat
Gold Museum, Ballarat, Victoria

Blacksmith's tools and branding iron made by Tom Wilson about 1890
Gatton Historical Society, Queensland

Plough made by Tom Wilson 1890
private collection

Tram advertising sign for Brennans 1920s
Eastern Goldfields Historical Society, Boulder, Western Australia

Daily ledger, tins and food packages from Brennan and Geraghty's store 1880s–1910
National Trust of Queensland

Golden lift gates from Mark Foy's Sydney emporium 1935
Powerhouse Museum, Sydney, gift of New South Wales Department of Public Works, 1989

Wrapping paper carrying the famous Mark Foy's jingle 1930s
private collection

Dress bought from TC Beirne and worn at the Spinsters' Ball 1930s
Powerhouse Museum, Sydney, gift of Sue Watson, 1988

Literature

Vincent Buckley's writing desk and personal effects
on loan from Penelope Buckley

Unpublished draft, 'Going to Ireland' 1960s
by Vincent Buckley
National Library of Australia

The Chronicles of Early Melbourne, 1835 to 1852 **(Vol. 1)** 1888
by Edmund Finn ('Garryowen')
published by Fergusson and Mitchell, Melbourne
National Library of Australia

Book of handwritten poems belonging to exiled Fenian rebel John Boyle O'Reilly 1869
State Library of Western Australia

Bring Larks and Heroes 1967
by Thomas Keneally
published by Cassell Australia
on loan from Thomas Keneally

Edmund Duggan's actor's wig about 1912
National Library of Australia

Original script by Edmund Duggan for *The Burke and Wills Expedition of 1860* 1916
National Film and Sound Archive

Alice Guerin Crist's handwritten manuscript of 'Mother and the fairy folk'
on loan from Dimity Dornan

When Rody Came to Ironbark and Other Verses 1927
by Alice Guerin Crist
Cornstalk Publishing Company, Sydney
on loan from Richard Reid

Ethel Florence Lindesay ('Henry Handel') Richardson's Varityper typewriter 1930s
State Library of Victoria

A continuing presence

The craic

Golden Guitar awarded to Ted Egan for 'Drover's boy' 2000
on loan from Ted Egan

One of Slim Dusty's signature hats
on loan from Leon Concannon

Poster, 'Slim Dusty Show: The seven gold record man coming your way'
on loan from Joy Kirkpatrick

Billy Moran's accordion 1953
on loan from Eileen Moran

Australian Folk Trust Award presented to Billy Moran 1996
on loan from Eileen Moran

Mick Doherty's fiddle
on loan from Mick Doherty

National Folk Recording Award 2008
on loan from Trouble in the Kitchen

Golden Fiddle Award for Best Album, Tamworth 2009
on loan from Trouble in the Kitchen

Irish dancing dress made by Kathryn Trenholme 2010
on loan from Kathryn Trenholme

Queensland Irish Association Pipe Band kilt, cap, belt and Tara brooch 1990s
on loan from Colin Ennis, Queensland Irish Association Pipe Band

Framed photograph of Irish dancers and piper about 1900–1920
Irish National Association, Sydney

Framed photograph of an Irish dancer about 1900–1920
Irish National Association, Sydney

Statuette of Thomas Moore with lyre 1853
by John Hogan
National Gallery of Ireland, Dublin

Song sheet, 'The last rose of summer', from *Moore's Selection of Irish Melodies No. 5* 1870–79
National Library of Australia

Uillean pipes belonging to John Shaw Wayland 1780s
School of Music, University of Western Australia

Medallion awarded to Irish piper John Wayland by the people of Geraldton, Western Australia, for services to the community during the First World War 1916
Irish Traditional Music Archive, Dublin

Memorial harp, made by Paddy Meehan, Brisbane 1990s
Queensland Irish Association

Oliver Goldsmith's walking stick flute about 1750s
Irish Traditional Music Archive, Dublin

Beale player piano (pianola) and stool 1926
National Museum of Australia

Monstrance 1928
on loan from Peter and Maureen Dunham

Josie O'Shea's prayer book, purchased in Ireland 1928
on loan from Peter and Maureen Dunham

Licensee sign for the Borroloola Hotel 1945
on loan from Peter and Maureen Dunham

Arklow Total Abstinence Society medallion 1830s
National Museum of Ireland, Dublin

'Mrs 'Arris & Mrs 'Iggs', Toohey's advertising poster 1934
Powerhouse Museum, Sydney, purchased 2004

Toohey's green beer bottle about 1910–1920s
Powerhouse Museum, Sydney, gift of Bob Edmunds, 1988

Mild Bitter Ale bottle 1930s
Toohey's Brewery, Sydney

Mash tun brass wheel for brewing 1950s
Toohey's Brewery, Sydney

Cooper's tool 1950s
Toohey's Brewery, Sydney

Irish in sport

Mourning locket, belonging to boxer Les Darcy's sweetheart, Winnie O'Sullivan, containing a photograph of Darcy and a lock of his hair 1917
National Museum of Australia

Larry Foley's boxing belt trophy 1880s
NSW Hall of Champions, Sydney Olympic Park

Horseshoe memento of Tommy Corrigan 1894
Australian Racing Museum, Melbourne

Silver cup awarded to Fanny Durack by Longsight Swimming Club, Manchester, for winning the 100 yards invitation scratch race in 'English record time' 29 July 1912
NSW Hall of Champions, Sydney Olympic Park

Jim Stynes's Melbourne Football Club jersey 1998
on loan from Jim Stynes

Melbourne Cup won by Vintage Crop 1993
on loan from Dr Michael Smurfit

Jockey silks worn by Michael Kinane, rider of Vintage Crop 1993
on loan from Dr Michael Smurfit

Tadhg Kennelly's Sydney Swans premiership medallion 2005
on loan from Tadhg Kennelly

Tadhg Kennelly's All Ireland Senior Football Championship jersey 2009
on loan from Tadhg Kennelly

James Parker's hurling stick before 1914
on loan from Michael Parker

Poem about hurling 1920s
on loan from Michael Parker

Irish-Australian Athletic Association Football Challenge Trophy 1950s
Gaelic Athletic Association Victoria, Melbourne

Reconnecting with Ireland

Medal sent to Sister Brenda Browne by the President of Ireland on the occasion of her 103rd birthday 2008
The Mercy Heritage Centre, Brisbane

Letter of congratulations from the President of Ireland 2008
The Mercy Heritage Centre, Brisbane

Backpack about 2000
on loan from Pauline Maloney

Currachs 2010
by Kiera O'Toole
on loan from the artist

Basket made by John Moriarty's mother 1950s
on loan from John Moriarty

Model of the Qantas *Wunala Dreaming* aircraft 1994
National Museum of Australia

Fishing rod belonging to John Moriarty's father 1928
on loan from John Moriarty

3EA T-shirt 1970s
on loan from Claire Dunne

2EA ID tag 1970s
on loan from Claire Dunne

Medal of the Order of Australia 1999
on loan from Claire Dunne

Claire Dunne's chair cover from the set of *They're a Weird Mob* 1966
on loan from Claire Dunne

First edition of the *Irish Exile* 1988
on loan from Billy Cantwell

Nyomi Horgan's Rose of Tralee winner's dress 1995
Rose of Tralee International Festival Organisation

Nyomi Horgan's Rose of Tralee winner's sash 1995
on loan from Nyomi Horgan

Lisa Manning's Rose of Tralee winner's dress 2001
Rose of Tralee International Festival Organisation

Lisa Manning's Rose of Tralee winner's sash 2001
on loan from Lisa Manning (Parkinson)

Kathryn Feeney's Rose of Tralee winner's dress 2006
Rose of Tralee International Festival Organisation

Kathryn Feeney's Rose of Tralee winner's sash and crown 2006
on loan from Kathryn Feeney

St Patrick's Day

St Patrick's Day banner 1960s
Celtic Club, Melbourne

St Patrick's Day badges 1920s
private collection

St Patrick's Day badge 1920s
Loreto College, Adelaide

St Patrick's Day themed hats and green wig 2008–10
on loan from Arron Madelly

Story circle

Conditional pardon granted to John Crinigan 1849
on loan from Marilyn Folger

Ned Ryan's certificate of freedom and leather wallet 1830s
St Clement's Retreat and Conference Centre, Galong, New South Wales

Isabella Mary Kelly's 'MK' and 'K' branding irons about 1830s
on loan from Geoff Boyle

Jug depicting 'John Lawless Esqre / Order of Liberators' 19th century
on loan from Michael and Stephanie Lawless and family

Gold brooch presented to Lola Montez 28 December 1855
private collection

Lola Montez Doing the 'Spider Dance' 1855
by John Michael Skipper
State Library of South Australia

The Bagot Cup 1859
made by Charles Edward Firnhaber
Kapunda Historical Society, South Australia

Father Ted Kennedy's replica penal cross, ceramic cross and shillelagh (Irish club)
on loan from Sister Marnie Kennedy

Sir Richard Bourke's map case early 19th century
on loan from Seamus Flynn

Sir Richard Bourke's ceremonial or dress sword 1830s
State Library of New South Wales

Letters of instruction from Queen Victoria to Governor George Ferguson Bowen 1859
Queensland Parliamentary Library, Brisbane

Governor George Ferguson Bowen's ceremonial or dress sword 1860s
State Library of Queensland, Brisbane

Engraved cigarette case given to Captain Francis de Groot, who famously slashed the ribbon at the opening ceremony of the Sydney Harbour Bridge 1932
State Library of New South Wales

Scissors used by New South Wales Premier Jack Lang to cut the re-joined ribbon at the opening ceremony of the Sydney Harbour Bridge 1932
Parliament of New South Wales, Sydney

Victoria Cross awarded to Private Martin O'Meara, 16th Battalion, AIF 1916
Army Museum of Western Australia, Fremantle

O'Meara's 'Rising Sun' collar badge about 1915
Australian War Memorial

Narrbong **(string bags)** 2010
by Lorraine Connelly-Northey
on loan from the artist

Defiance flour bag early 20th century
Cobb & Co Museum, Toowoomba, Queensland

Defiance microwave cake mix 1990
Powerhouse Museum, Sydney, gift of Packaging Council of Australia, 1991

Visitors' book, Irish Legation in Australia 1946
Embassy of Ireland, Canberra

Gold probe supposedly used on the Duke of Edinburgh to remove a bullet following an assassination attempt March 1868
Royal Prince Alfred Hospital Museum, Sydney

Women's suffrage petition organised by Mary Lee, presented to the South Australian parliament 1894
South Australian Parliament

Prime ministers

Gold cigarette case presented to Prime Minister Stanley Melbourne Bruce by the Duke and Duchess of York 9 May 1927
National Archives of Australia

Silver loving-cup presented to Prime Minister Joseph Lyons by the Irish government 1935
National Trust Tasmania

Scrapbook belonging to Prime Minister Joseph Lyons about 1935
National Library of Australia

Commission signed by King George V appointing Sir Isaac Isaacs to be Governor-General and Commander-in-Chief of Australia 18 December 1930
National Library of Australia

'Freedom of the City of London' scroll presented to Prime Minister James Scullin 4 November 1930
Parliament House Gift Collection, Parliament House Art Collection, Department of Parliamentary Services, Canberra

'United for Victory' jigsaw depicting President Franklin D Roosevelt and Prime Minister John Curtin 1941
Australian War Memorial

Relic from the London Blitz presented to Prime Minister John Curtin by the House of Commons 1941
presented to the Department of the Parliamentary Library and the People of Australia by the British House of Commons Library
Parliament House Gift Collection, Parliament House Art Collection, Department of Parliamentary Services, Canberra

Hall display

Union Combine Harvester 1890s
made by Nicholson and Morrow
Wimmera–Mallee Pioneer Museum,
Jeparit, Victoria

Furphy water cart 1900s
made by J Furphy and Sons, Shepparton,
Victoria
Australian War Memorial, Canberra

Irish side (or jaunting) car mid-20th
century
on loan from Tommy Doherty

Wolseley 1500 saloon 1959
National Museum of Australia

Irish *currach* 1996
made by Johnny Jimmy McDonagh, Aran
Islands
on loan from Paddy Macdonald

The Paddy Hannan Memorial Statue
1929
by John MacLeod
Kalgoorlie-Boulder Council, Western
Australia

**Section of locking-bar water
pipeline** early 1900s
Water Corporation, Western Australia

Acknowledgements

This exhibition is about a story – the story of the Irish in Australia – which has reached into nearly every aspect of our national life since 1788. It could not have been put together without the enthusiastic cooperation of individuals who manage personal, local and institutional collections right across Australia, and in Ireland, the United States and New Zealand. The National Museum of Australia is grateful to all of them. In a real sense, this is their exhibition.

From the beginning the Ambassador for Ireland, His Excellency Máirtín Ó Fainín, and his staff at the Embassy of Ireland have given us constant support. This has been vital for liaison with the Irish community throughout Australia, as well as with significant organisations and institutions in Ireland. There we established a close and important working relationship with the National Museum of Ireland and its director, Dr Patrick Wallace. The willingness of Irish museums, galleries and individuals to entrust us with their material has been essential for the development of the exhibition.

Every object in this exhibition is important, but some are vital in telling the story of the Irish in Australia. The State Library of Victoria, the Police Museum (Victoria) and a private lender have made it possible to display all four suits of Kelly gang armour for the first time at a national institution. The Public Record Office Victoria has allowed Duffy's land map, probably Australia's largest map, to be included in the exhibition, and the Catholic Church has been generous in making magnificent objects available from diocesan and convent collections nationwide. In Canberra, the National Library of Australia, the National Gallery of Australia, the National Archives of Australia and the Australian War Memorial have all provided invaluable support.

We owe special thanks to Dr Val Noone (Melbourne) who gave invaluable guidance and assistance in searching out material, and in providing feedback and advice generally. Exhibition consultant Dr Ann Herraman (Adelaide) went well beyond the call of duty in helping to find key objects in South Australia. In the Kimberley, Andrew Barker of the Kununurra Historical Society made it possible to tell the story of Irish pastoralists in the region. Associate Professor Jeff Brownrigg (University of Canberra), Dr Siobhan McHugh (University of Wollongong), Dr Michael McKernan (Canberra) and Brendon Kelson (Canberra) also gave willingly of their time. Many others – far too many to name here – have contributed generously of their time and knowledge and we owe a debt to them all.

The Museum would also like to acknowledge the History Channel for its support and generous contribution in being the major sponsor for the exhibition.

Additional thanks is due to Culture Ireland, Ireland Abroad, Tourism Ireland, Enterprise Ireland, The Heraldry and Genealogy Society of Canberra Inc., the Lansdowne Club, the Irish and Celtic clubs and the Irish heritage and cultural associations around Australia who have offered advice and support for this exhibition.

The members of the National Irish Business Association of Canberra have pursued the idea of an exhibition on the Irish in Australia for many years. Their hopes have now been realised.